COLORADO
ELEVATIONS

NEW HEIGHTS IN COLORADO COOKING

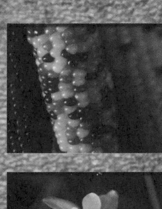

Conifer Newcomers and Neighbors is a women's
organization whose mission is to support our community, welcome
new residents, and introduce them to mountain living. Its purpose is
exclusively educational, social, and charitable.

Library of Congress Control Number: 2006905094

ISBN: 0-9786287-0-5

First Edition, First Printing:
2000 copies, October, 2006

This cookbook is a collection of favorite recipes,
which are not necessarily all original recipes.

WIMMER
COOKBOOKS

A CONSOLIDATED GRAPHICS COMPANY

800.548.2537   wimmerco.com

Sponsors

We would like to recognize the generosity of these wonderful Colorado businesses and individuals who contributed financially to this project. Their confidence in us is truly appreciated, and their support of our community projects makes them truly special.

Premier

Pinnacle

EVERGREEN
newspapers

AIR SCIENCES INC.

training & consulting

MOUNTAIN
CONNECTION

Eye Consultants of Colorado

Colleen and Vance Andrus

Peak

Caren Matteucci
King Soopers
Marvena Baker-Shriver

Promontory

Aspen Specialty Foods & Catering
Phil Campbell, State Farm Insurance Agency
Conifer Village Hardware and Sporting Goods
Chipotle Mexican Grill, Inc.
Mountain Handbell Coalition, Mountain Ringers,
Evergreen/Conifer

Salon Foushee & Day Spa
The Kitchen and Bath Center
Treadstone Interiors
Ellen Weissmann
Meme & Doc Hardin
Grant Automotive
Patrick & Marilyn Flanigan

Photography Credits

CARROLL BOSSIEUX

Carroll is a native of California, but has made Colorado her home since 1978. She joined Conifer Newcomers & Neighbors in 2000. She loves gardening, reading and photography.

ANN COBB

Ann moved to Conifer in 1995 after living most of her life in New York and New England. She is an avid photographer and has a great love for hiking and the outdoors. The spectacular beauty of Colorado has provided many photo opportunities in the state that she truly loves.

LYLE CURRIER

Lyle is a Colorado native but has also lived in Arizona and Wyoming. He has traveled widely and developed his interest in photography amid the diverse and beautiful locations during those travels, capturing those moments of light or ambience that create a special connection. He has received awards at several juried art shows and exhibits.

ANNETTE SNODGRASS

It was the love of the outdoors (and the US Air Force) that brought Annette and her camera to Colorado from the Midwest 25 years ago. After her military service, Annette moved to the foothills and now resides in Conifer. Whether it's the joy of a sunny field of wildflowers or the quiet solitude of a snowy winter day, photography gives her a way to share that beauty with others.

JEANIE YOUNG

Jeanie is the owner of Young's Photography and has been carrying a camera by her side for over 20 years. She currently lives in Conifer but spent many years abroad in Asia and Europe. She is an avid nature photographer and also a gourmet cook with contributions of both photographs and recipes.

3

Dedications

Thanks to Sam (Pop) and Jenny Ainsworth for bringing us to Conifer and to our kids Elizabeth, Laurel and Alex. Thanks, Mom, for your cooking. *~Aimee Ainsworth*

For my wonderful family and friends, who understand what it means to be a Cajun at heart: "What an incredible meal that was! Where are we going to eat next?" *~Ashley Andrus*

With love to my mother, Freda, who knows and shares the recipe for family love, who masterfully crafts the best meals ever and for whom I clean my plate. *~Marvena Baker-Shriver*

To honor the volunteers and staff of Mountain Resource Center who are neighbors helping neighbors through their many contributions to our community. Mountain Resource Center appreciates each of you! *~Marvena Baker-Shriver*

My thanks to all the women (grandmothers, mothers-in-law, stepmother, friends and Mom) who taught me to cook. *~Carroll Bossieux*

To my family, friends and "Ya-Ya's." There's nothing like sharing a great meal with the people you cherish! *~Randi Brattin*

To my family and friends who love to cook. May you find new recipes to enjoy and share with others. *~Melsande Clayton*

To Lois Currier, a Conifer ranch woman of indominitable spirit who developed many recipes while living in the Yellow Barn house and whose love was shared in her cooking. *~Colleen Currier*

To all my friends who have made getting together around a meal a great and wonderful experience! *~Rev. Beth Graham*

In memory of Ella Lieux, who ruled our home and kitchen in New Roads, Louisiana. At 4´11˝ tall she was nicknamed "The Sergeant," "Sarge" for short, by her children, nieces, nephews and neighborhood kids. This nickname stuck the rest of her life. *~Meme Hardin*

For Grandma Jones — she cooked on the same coal stove for over 50 years. *~Chris Hollis*

In memory of Helen Manfredini: mother, grandmother, great-grandmother. You made our lives richer with your love and your incredible cooking. You are greatly missed. *~Sue Hosier*

Thanks to CN&N for their continuing support of our Conifer community. *~Jarvis Construction*

Non-cooks unite! *~Vicki Joyce*

Dedicated to my mother, Barbara Spriestersbach. She always made homemade cookies and bread. Being an ungrateful child, I longed for Oreos and Wonder Bread. Fortunately I grew up! *~Susan Lapidus*

Dedicated to my husband who loves to cook and my daughter who is always hungry. ~Jill Lovell

Nancy, your love continues to nourish me after all this time. ~Alex Matteucci

Mom and Dad, you taught me why to cook, as much as how.
~Caren Matteucci

Dedicated to both of my mothers, Ann McAtee and Mary Tipton. Both wonderful ladies served their communities with enthusiasm and dedication to helping others whenever they were asked. With love, ~Bonnie McAtee

To my mother, Juanita Odishooe, who taught me how to cook at a very young age and is the best chef I know! From your loving daughter. ~Sondra McBride

In memory of my mom, Catherine Pominski, who always took pleasure in her cooking, especially the crab dip she traditionally made for Christmas Eve service at her church. ~Cathy McCloskey

For my friend, Nita Alspaugh. We had great fun with Josh, our shared grandson. ~Melba Neel

To "Mudder," my sister, Karrie Kay Howard, and Lisa Kay, the family gourmet cooks. To Patty Archer, best friend and world famous chocolate chip cookie maker. Much love, ~Judy Ramsay

To my "quick cook" Mom, Judy, whose "Angel Eggs" are the hit of La Junta's social events and whose chocolate cake contains a little coffee and a lot of love. ~Don Shriver

For my mom, Betty Sable, 96 and retired from the kitchen. She says she never liked the kitchen, but we always knew where to go for a great meal, served with love. ~Barbara Smith

In fond memory of "Packer," our Portuguese Water Dog, who loved everyone, lived life to the fullest and enjoyed eating, especially homemade treats. ~Mary Sosnowski

Dedicated with love to all the great cooks in my family: Mother, Dad & Miss Ellie, Man-ma, Aunt Gerry, Aunt Jessie, and especially Bummie. ~Victoria Sparer

Live Well! Eat Well! Celebrate Life! ~Rebecca Swain

Bernice, Jeanne, Louise, Johanna — Four generations of cheesecake queens. From sea level to 8500 feet, this smooth concoction satisfies our souls...long may it touch yours. ~Louise Ullmann

My "Reen" — You encourage us all to be the best we can be; you raise the bar on "Human." Thanks for being you...my "Reen." ~Louise Ullmann

For my mom, Nancy Brown, who loves my cooking. ~Jeanie Young

Cookbook Committee

CHAIR: Caren Matteucci
CO-CHAIR: Mary Kennelly

COMMITTEE MEMBERS:

Colleen Andrus	Meme Lieux Hardin	Victoria Sparer
Ashley Andrus	Laura Penland	Thresea Stimatze
Randi Brattin	Nancy Pfohl	Louise Ullmann
Lorraine Garver	Barbara Smith	Jeanie Young

OTHER VOLUNTEER ASSISTANCE:

Marvena Baker-Shriver	Valerie Grant	Connie Powell
Ann Cobb	Christina Jensen	Sareth Prum
Sue Diabate	Kevin Lewis	Jan Swenson
	Karen Nelson	Nancy Traszyneki
	Kim McCallum	

6

CONTRIBUTORS:

Aimee Ainsworth	Carol Fabbri	Chris Leonard	Judy Ramsay
Ashley Andrus	Marilyn Flanigan	Cheri Lepro	Sandra Richardson
Colleen Andrus	Linda Lieux Fontenot	Venicia Mason	Colleen Roccanova
Lori Andrus	Lawrence French	Caren Matteucci	Cindy Russell
Shannon Andrus	Lorraine Garver	Richard Matteucci	Alice Scarborough
Vance Andrus	Gaye Gilbert	Becky Maupin	Joyce Schindler
Andrea Arnason	Carol Glasby	Bonnie McAtee	Betty Senff
Cindy Aron	Beth Graham	Sondra McBride	Barbara Smith
Julie Auch	Valerie Grant	Kim McCallum	Dawn Smith
Marvena Baker-Shriver	Charlene Hahn	Cathy McCloskey	Mary Sosnowski
Sharon Bonomo	Gisele Hall	Jane McDaniel	Victoria Sparer
Carroll Bossieux	Grant Hardin	Emily Miller	Thresea Stimatze
Randi Brattin	Meme Lieux Hardin	Betty Mitchell	Jan Swenson
Lydia Brown	William Hardin, MD	Susan Morris	Alice Szwarce
Vi Brown	Joyce Haried	Harriet Mullin	Laurie Taylor
Kat Buscombe	Lee Heideman	Eva Murray	Ed Tinkey
Shirley Castro	Sharon Hollis	Kathy Nabarrete	Sue Tinkey
Mel Clayton	Toni Holte	Ellen Naylor	Joy Travis
Linda Clopton	Richard Hood	Melba Neel	Louise Ullmann
Ann Cobb	Sue Hosier	Dee O'Day	Toni Venables
Diane Corso	Bobbie Houston	Laurel Ostberg	Jane Francis Ward
Steve Croft	Sherri Hurd	Christian Patrick	Joann Watts
Colleen Currier	Terri Itzig	Dalene Pauls	Ellen Weissmann
Lee Curry	Terry Jarvis	Monique Pauls	Terri White
Linda DeHoff	Christina Jensen	Laura Penland	Elaine Wilbanks
Pat DePasture	Janis Johnson	Brigitte Peterson	Barbara Wingate
Katie Dix	Victoria (Vicki) Joyce	Nancy Pfohl	Bettiann Witulski
Julie Donelson	Kathy Kramer	Nancy Picton	Jeanie Young
Billie Eaton	Susan Lapidus	Andrew Powell	
	Sherry Law	Connie Powell	

Foreword
el·ó·vā·shən NOUN:

1. a. The act or an instance of elevating.

    b. The condition of being elevated.

2. An elevated place or position.

3. The height to which something is elevated above a point of reference such as the ground.

4. Loftiness of thought or feeling.

5. The height of a thing above a reference level; altitude.

Living in the mountains of Colorado is extraordinary and cooking is no exception. Cooking is affected by many things: your state of mind, the type of recipe, the quality of ingredients, the occasion, and your physical surroundings. Mountain style cooking embodies all of those attributes and creates its own unique setting. The collection of recipes in *Elevations* will lift your spirits, delight your family and guests, and raise their culinary compliments to new heights.

Colorado cooking styles are for those who enjoy good food and fresh air. Blue skies and granite peaks have a way of making you hungry.

7

Introduction

Colorado is a state of contrasts. Its distinctive seasons, breathtaking scenery and diverse cities and towns make it a wonderful place to live and to visit. You can drive from windswept prairies to snowcapped peaks in about an hour. You can leave work in Denver and be on your deck in Conifer at 9000 feet in less time than that. Those attractions and many others have drawn visitors and new residents each year to Colorado and to Conifer.

Colorado's people represent those same contrasts. It is often said that "No one's from Colorado...they all moved here from someplace else." That is an exaggeration, but it is accurate that many who call Colorado home moved here from other states and countries. This mix of diverse backgrounds and hometowns gives Colorado a unique flavor and lifestyle. Conifer, the foothills community outside of Denver that we call home, has that special quality of life that results from living where you want and loving where you live.

Conifer is one of several foothills communities southwest of the Denver metropolitan area. The Front Range of the Rockies surges upward next to the Denver skyline and marks the boundary between urban life and mountain living. Life up here is different. Elk, deer and other wildlife are abundant; the evergreens conceal homes in every valley and mountainside. Water and topsoil are precious; government services are limited. National forests and the Continental Divide are our vistas.

The 160 members of Conifer Newcomers and Neighbors are as diverse as Colorado. Our members hail from all over the U.S. and several foreign countries. CN&N often serves as an entry point to our close-knit community for new residents, and they find someone who shares their same memories and interests. New friendships are formed, and the community gains another family. Our collection of recipes are representative of that diversity and a love of good food.

We have discovered how beneficial it is to have different viewpoints and talents within an organization. Fresh ideas and energy contribute to the group's vitality. For 35 years CN&N has raised funds to benefit local charitable organizations, schools, service providers and other community groups. *Elevations* is an extension of those fundraising efforts. All proceeds from this cookbook project will be awarded to worthy causes serving those in our community and will enable us to provide more assistance to those groups.

Eligible groups submit funding requests to us each year. The list of beneficiaries is a long one. CN&N has assisted in preserving open space, enabled students to enjoy broader educational experiences, purchased needed equipment for our firefighters, funded programs to help our area crisis center and family resource programs, supported programs for pets and wildlife protection, contributed to a playground for community youth, volunteered and supported the arts and arts programming, and many other worthwhile community services. A partial listing of past beneficiaries includes: Mountain Resource Center, Park Country Crisis Center, Beaver Ranch Community, area schools and fire departments, arts groups and many others.

Providing support and funding for causes like those above is a worthy pursuit. Conifer Newcomers & Neighbors is proud of its accomplishments in our community. We hope you will share that wonderful feeling of accomplishment each time you use this book to prepare a recipe and remember that this project will continue to enhance the lives of many in our community. Enjoy!   *~CN&N Cookbook Committee*

Table of Contents

9

10

APPETIZERS

Contents

Sherried Crab Dip

4	tablespoons butter
4	tablespoons flour
1	pint half-and-half or cream
4	tablespoons sherry
	Salt to taste
	Red pepper to taste
1	pound crabmeat
1	cup sharp Cheddar cheese, grated

Make cream sauce in top of double boiler by combining butter, flour, and half-and-half and warming over medium heat. Add sherry, salt, and red pepper to taste. Remove from heat. Add crabmeat and cheese, stirring until cheese melts. Keep warm in chafing dish. Do not overcook.

Serves 4-6

Seafood Dip

1	envelope vegetable soup mix
16	ounces sour cream
½-¾	cup mayonnaise
6	ounces softened cream cheese
2	tablespoons lemon juice
	Hot sauce to taste
8	ounces artichoke hearts
	Creole seasoning to taste
1	tablespoon sherry
1	teaspoon Worcestershire sauce
1-2	cups shredded Cheddar (or combination of Monterey Jack and Cheddar)
2	pounds seafood: crabmeat, imitation crab, or shrimp
	Cooking spray

Preheat oven to 325°F. Spray 8x8-inch glass casserole with cooking spray. Thoroughly combine all ingredients and place in casserole dish. Bake uncovered for 30 minutes or until heated through. Sprinkle more Cheddar on top if desired. When it has been bubbling for about 5 minutes, remove from oven. Dip will thicken as it cools. Serve with French bread slices or crackers.

Serves 6-8

> To slice or grate cheese more easily, chill in freezer about 10 minutes before slicing.

Olive Tapenade

20	pitted kalamata olives, chopped
1	tablespoon chopped capers, rinsed and drained
1	teaspoon olive oil
½	teaspoon anchovy paste
	Fresh cracked pepper

Mix all ingredients well and serve with crackers or bread.

Serves: 4

Variation: Add ⅛ cup crumbled feta and/or Greek olives.

14

Hummus

1	15.5-ounce can chickpeas
2	cloves garlic
4	tablespoons fresh lemon juice
¼	cup olive oil
½	cup tahini paste
¼	cup water
	Salt, pepper, red pepper (optional)

Blend chickpeas and garlic in food processor. Add lemon juice and olive oil. Process until smooth. In a separate bowl, combine tahini paste and water with a fork until smooth. Add to chickpeas. Process until combined and smooth. This can easily be altered by adding roasted red peppers, sun-dried tomatoes or jalapeño peppers to taste.

Serve with pita wedges, sugar snap peas and crackers. This is a great appetizer to take to a party and makes a great camping snack as well.

Serves 4-6

Balsamic Basil Salsa

2	medium tomatoes, chopped
1	tablespoon minced onion
¼	cup finely chopped basil
½	teaspoon minced jalapeño pepper
2	tablespoons balsamic vinegar
1	tablespoon olive oil

Stir all ingredients together and refrigerate for 30 minutes. Serve with tortilla chips.

Serves 4-6

White Bean Hummus

2   garlic cloves
1   teaspoon chopped fresh
       rosemary
2   15.5-ounce cans Great
       Northern beans, rinsed and
       drained
3   tablespoons lemon juice
3   tablespoons tahini
¾   teaspoon salt
¼   teaspoon ground red pepper
¼   cup olive oil
       Paprika for garnish (optional)

Blend garlic and rosemary in a food processor until minced. Add beans, lemon juice, tahini, salt, and red pepper. Process until smooth, stopping to scrape down sides. Gradually pour olive oil through food chute with processor running. Process until mixture is smooth. May add water to increase smoothness of consistency. Cover and chill 1 hour. Garnish with paprika if desired. Serve with crackers, sliced cucumber, pimiento-stuffed olives, and pitted kalamata olives. Makes 3 cups.

Serves 6-8

15

Guacamole

2   avocados, peeled and chopped
       or mashed
1   plum tomato, chopped
1-2 cloves garlic, minced
¼   cup chopped onion, white
       or red
       Fresh ground pepper
       Sea salt
       Dash red pepper
¼   teaspoon cumin
       Juice of one lemon

For chunky guacamole, chop everything pretty coarsely, or chop more finely for a smoother consistency. Mix the avocado, tomato, garlic and onion, then add spices to taste. Mix in a little bit of lemon juice both for taste and to keep it from turning brown. Serve with tortilla chips.

Serves 4-6

The fun part of this recipe is varying the ingredients. It can be a little different every time, but should always taste really fresh.

Guacamole with Jalapeño Peppers

4-5 avocados, mashed
½ cup white onion, chopped
1 large tomato, chopped
3 jalapeño peppers, halved, seeded, and chopped
¼ teaspoon cilantro
Onion and garlic salt to taste
Juice of 3 limes

Mix all ingredients together. To retain color, leave 2 avocado pits in mixture until serving. Serve with tortilla chips.

Serves 4-6

Cranberry Orange Cheese Spread

1 8-ounce package cream cheese, softened
2 tablespoons concentrated orange juice
⅛ teaspoon cinnamon
1 tablespoon sugar
¼ teaspoon orange zest
¼ cup finely chopped dried cranberries
¼ cup finely chopped pecans (optional)

In an electric mixer bowl, combine the cream cheese, concentrated orange juice, cinnamon, and sugar on medium speed until smooth. Fold in orange zest, cranberries, and pecans. Refrigerate 1-2 hours or overnight. Remove from fridge and let warm up a little before serving, so it's easier to spread. Garnish with cranberries or orange slices. Serve with crackers.

Serves 4-6

Keep a pack of unflavored dental floss in the kitchen. It is often better than a knife to cleanly cut all kinds of soft foods, soft cheese, rolled dough, layered cake and cheesecake.

Southwest Onion Dip

4   slices yellow onion, about ½ inch thick

Extra virgin olive oil

½   cup loosely packed, fresh cilantro leaves, with some stems

½   cup sour cream

4   tablespoons pine nuts

4   tablespoons cream cheese

2   teaspoons fresh lime juice

1   teaspoon kosher salt

1   teaspoon granulated onion

1   teaspoon chili powder

1   teaspoon granulated garlic

¼   teaspoon ground cumin

¼   teaspoon freshly ground black pepper

4-6 10-inch flour tortillas

Brush or spray both sides of onion slices with olive oil. Grill onion slices on BBQ grill until marked and very tender, about 15 minutes, turn once halfway through grilling time. Put the onion slices in a food processor, add the remaining ingredients except the tortillas, and pulse into a smooth purée, scraping down the sides of the bowl occasionally. Transfer to a serving bowl.

Grill tortillas until crisp and browned in spots, 3-5 minutes, turning once halfway through the grilling time (this can also be done by placing the tortillas in a hot cast iron skillet). Cut each tortilla into eight wedges, and serve with the dip.

Serves 4

Pumpkin Dip for Sliced Apples

¾   cup (six ounces) reduced-fat cream cheese at room temperature

⅓   cup packed brown sugar

1   tablespoon pure maple syrup

½   teaspoon ground cinnamon

¼   teaspoon ground nutmeg

Dash of cloves

½   cup of canned pumpkin

24-36 apple slices about ¼ inch thick (two apples)

Lemon juice

Beat cream cheese, brown sugar, maple syrup, and spices until smooth. Add pumpkin and mix until blended. Cover and chill for at least 30 minutes. Slice unpeeled apples and store in plastic bag with lemon juice to prevent browning until ready to use. Arrange apples on a plate with pumpkin dip in a bowl in the center.

Serves 10-12

Use Pacific Rose or Gala apples, or Granny Smith apples for a more tart taste.

A very good autumn appetizer; nutritious and low-calorie.

Cajun Mushrooms

20	large mushrooms or 40 smaller mushrooms
1	large onion
1	large bell pepper
1	celery stalk
1	stick butter
1	pound crabmeat
¼	cup lemon juice
⅓	cup chopped green onions
⅓	cup chopped parsley
1¼	cups breadcrumbs
1¼	tablespoons Worcestershire sauce
1	tablespoon hot sauce
1	tablespoon salt
1⅔	teaspoons red pepper
⅓	teaspoon black pepper
⅓	teaspoon white pepper
2½	tablespoons Vermouth

Preheat oven to 375°F. Remove stems from mushrooms and wipe the caps. Chop onion, bell pepper, and celery finely and sauté in butter until soft. Stir in crabmeat and remaining ingredients, and simmer for 10 minutes. Remove from heat and let cool. Generously stuff mushroom caps with the dressing. Place in single layers on an ovenproof dish and bake for 15 minutes. Makes 20 large mushrooms or 40 small mushrooms.

Serves 6-12

Jalapeño Poppers

1	8-ounce package softened cream cheese
1	cup shredded sharp Cheddar cheese
1	cup shredded Monterey Jack cheese
6	bacon strips, cooked and crumbled
¼	teaspoon salt
¼	teaspoon chili powder
¼	teaspoon garlic powder
1	pound fresh jalapeños, halved lengthwise and seeded
½	cup dry bread crumbs
	Sour cream, onion dip, or ranch salad dressing

Preheat oven to 300°F. In a mixing bowl, combine the cheeses, bacon, and seasonings, mix well. Spoon about 2 tablespoons into each pepper half. Roll in bread crumbs. Place in a greased 15x10-inch baking pan. Bake uncovered for 20 minutes for spicy flavor, 30 minutes for medium flavor, or 40 minutes for mild flavor. Serve with sour cream, dip, or dressing. Makes about 2 dozen.

Serves 8-12

A
P
P
E
T
I
Z
E
R
S

When cutting or seeding hot peppers, use rubber or plastic gloves to protect your hands. Avoid touching eyes or face.

Prosciutto Stuffed Mushrooms

12 large fresh mushrooms
2   tablespoons butter
1   tablespoon olive oil
½   cup minced onion
1   garlic clove, minced
1   tablespoon chopped fresh
    parsley
1   teaspoon minced fresh
    marjoram (or ½ teaspoon
    dried)
1   cup bread crumbs
½   cup grated Parmesan cheese
½   cup chopped prosciutto or
    ham
1   teaspoon salt
¼   teaspoon pepper

Preheat oven to 350°F. Remove caps from mushrooms and set aside. Finely chop stems. In a medium frying pan, melt butter with olive oil over medium heat. Add onion and garlic and cook 2 to 3 minutes, or until onion is softened. Add mushroom stems and cook 3 minutes, or until mushroom liquid is exuded and then evaporates. Add parsley, marjoram, and bread crumbs. Cook 1 minute to combine. Stir in Parmesan cheese and prosciutto or ham. Season with salt and pepper. Stuff mushrooms, placing a mound of bread crumb mixture high in caps. Place in a buttered baking dish and bake 15 to 20 minutes, or until filling is crusty brown and mushroom caps are tender but still hold their shape.

Serves 6-8

Mushroom Crab Melts

3   bacon strips, diced
1   cup sliced fresh mushrooms
¼   cup chopped onion
1   6-ounce can crabmeat,
    drained, flaked and cartilage
    removed
1   cup shredded Swiss cheese
½   cup mayonnaise
⅓   cup grated Parmesan cheese
2   tablespoons softened butter or
    margarine
6   English muffins, split
    Dash cayenne pepper and
    paprika

Preheat oven to 400°F. Cook bacon in a skillet over medium heat until crisp, remove to paper towel. Drain skillet, reserving 2 tablespoons of drippings. Sauté mushrooms and onion in drippings until tender. In a large bowl, combine the crabmeat, Swiss cheese, mayonnaise, mushroom mixture, Parmesan cheese, and butter. Spread over muffin halves, sprinkle with cayenne and paprika. Place on an ungreased baking sheet. Bake for 10-15 minutes or until lightly browned. Cut into quarters to serve as hors d'oeuvres.

Serves 6

1 cup of chopped imitation crabmeat may be substituted for canned crabmeat.

Picante Cheese Squares

8　ounces sharp Cheddar cheese
8　ounces Monterey Jack cheese
3　eggs, beaten
½　cup picante sauce

Preheat oven to 350°F. Mix all ingredients and bake in ungreased 9x9-inch pan for 30 minutes. Blot off excess grease if necessary. Let cool and cut into bite-sized squares.

Serves 6-8

A
P
P
E
T
I
Z
E
R
S

Panko-Crusted Crab Cake Bites with Roasted Pepper Aïoli

ROASTED PEPPER AÏOLI
⅓　cup mayonnaise
¼　cup canned roasted red peppers, chopped and drained
1　tablespoon minced fresh chives
2　teaspoons lemon juice
1　teaspoon minced garlic

CRAB CAKE
¼　cup finely chopped celery
¼　cup finely chopped fresh chives
¼　cup mayonnaise
1　large egg
2　teaspoons Dijon mustard
¼　teaspoon hot sauce
12　ounces cooked and shelled crab
1¼　cups panko, divided
　　Fresh chives
　　Roasted pepper aïoli

To make the roasted pepper aïoli, mix all of the above ingredients in a small bowl. Blend or pulse in food processor until well combined. Refrigerate at least one hour or overnight.

Preheat oven to 475°F. In a large bowl, combine celery, minced chives, mayonnaise, egg, mustard and hot sauce; mix well. Stir crab and ¼ cup panko gently into mix. Put remaining panko in a shallow bowl. Shape crab mixture into 20 cakes about 2 inches wide and ½ inch thick. Turn each crab cake in the panko to coat. Press gently to make the crumbs adhere. Place cakes on an oiled baking sheet. Bake for 15 to 18 minutes until brown. Transfer crab cakes to a service platter and spoon a dollop of roasted pepper aïoli onto each crab cake. Garnish with fresh chives. Serve hot.

Serves 8-10

Panko are Japanese style bread crumbs and can be substituted with fine dried bread crumbs if needed.

Linda's Crawfish Pastries

½	cup chopped onions
¼	cup chopped green onions
3	stalks celery, finely chopped
3	tablespoons flour
1	stick plus 3 tablespoons butter
1	12-ounce can evaporated milk
⅓	pound processed cheese loaf
1	pound crawfish, chopped
1	egg yolk, slightly beaten
8	dozen frozen puff pastry shells

In a large skillet, sauté onions and celery in butter. Stir in flour. Remove from heat and slowly whisk in evaporated milk until the mixture thickens. Over medium heat, add cheese to this mixture and stir continuously until cheese is completely melted. Add egg yolks and crawfish. Bake pastry shells according to package directions. Serve hot crawfish mixture in warm shells.

Serves 24-32

This crawfish recipe is also great served in a chafing dish with Melba toast! Shrimp may be substituted for the crawfish.

Fiery Shrimp

½	cup celery tops
4	teaspoons salt
¼	cup mixed pickling spices
2½	pounds large shrimp, in shell
3	cups sliced sweet onions
7-8	bay leaves

SAUCE

1¼	cups vegetable oil
¾	cup white vinegar
1½	teaspoons salt
2½	teaspoons celery seed
	Black pepper to taste
1	small jar capers and juice
8-10	dashes hot sauce

In a large pot, heat enough water to cover shrimp. When it starts to boil, put in celery, salt, spices, and shrimp. After the water begins to boil again, cook 5 more minutes. Drain shrimp, cool with cold water. Peel and remove the black vein. Put cleaned shrimp and sliced onions in a large bowl that has a sealing cover. Add bay leaves. Make the sauce by mixing together all ingredients and pour over the shrimp and onions. Cover and store in the refrigerator for at least 24 hours. The longer it marinates, the better the flavor. Place shrimp and onions in a shallow dish and serve with saltine crackers. The onions are as good as the shrimp!

Serves 8-12

Scallops with Leeks and Garlic Oil

4 cups water

2¾ pounds leeks (white and light green parts, cut into ½-inch pieces)

8 tablespoons unsalted butter, divided

Ground nutmeg

Salt

1¾ pounds bay scallops

1 tablespoon chopped fresh thyme (or 1 teaspoon dried, crumbled)

Salt and pepper

4 tablespoons balsamic vinegar or red wine vinegar

3 large garlic cloves, chopped

¾ cup peanut oil

Bring water to boil in heavy medium saucepan. Add chopped leeks and cook until tender, about 10 minutes. Drain well, reserving leeks and liquid separately. Return liquid to saucepan. Boil until liquid is reduced to ½ cup, about 20 minutes.

Melt 4 tablespoons butter in heavy medium skillet over medium heat. Add leeks and sauté until golden, stirring occasionally, about 12 minutes. Season to taste with nutmeg and salt.

Melt remaining 4 tablespoons butter in another heavy medium skillet over medium high heat. Add scallops and thyme, season with salt and pepper. Sauté bay scallops until just cooked through, about 4 minutes. Using slotted spoon, transfer bay scallops to bowl. Add reduced leek cooking liquid to same skillet and boil until reduced to sauce consistency, about 3 minutes.

Pour reduced leek liquid into blender. Add balsamic vinegar and garlic cloves. With blender running, gradually pour in peanut oil. Season sauce to taste with salt and pepper.

To serve, gently warm everything. Arrange leeks on platter. Spoon scallops over the top. Drizzle generously with sauce. Serve extra sauce separately.

Serves 6-8

How to clean leeks: (1) Fill a long deep pan with water and add a few drops of lemon juice or wine vinegar. (2) Cut off the root end and the top few inches of green. (Most recipes call for only the white part, so save the green for the broth, if you like.) Slit each leek lengthwise, so it unscrolls. (3) Loosen the layers, and soak the leeks for about 10 minutes. Rinse well with fresh water and pat it dry with paper towels.

Teriyaki Chicken Wings

1	cup honey
½	cup soy sauce
2	tablespoons vegetable oil
2	tablespoons catsup
½	clove garlic, chopped
3	pounds chicken wings (preferably "drumettes")
	Salt and pepper to taste

Preheat oven to 375°F. Combine honey, soy sauce, vegetable oil, catsup, and garlic and whisk together. Place chicken in a shallow baking dish in a single layer. Salt and pepper wings. Pour sauce over wings. Bake for one hour. Turn after 30 minutes.

Serves 10-12

Chicken Chipotle Nachos with Cilantro Avocado Crème

CILANTRO AVOCADO CRÈME

⅓	cup mashed ripe avocado
2	tablespoons sour cream
1	tablespoon finely chopped fresh cilantro
2	teaspoons lime juice
2	teaspoons milk
	Salt and pepper to taste

NACHOS

1	tablespoon olive oil
½	cup chopped onions
½	teaspoon cumin seeds
½	teaspoon dried oregano
2	cans chipotle chilies
2	tablespoons tomato paste
1	tablespoon white wine vinegar
½	cup water
2	cups cooked and shredded chicken
24	corn tortilla chips
1½	cups shredded Monterey Jack cheese

To make the Cilantro Avocado Crème, mix all of the ingredients together in a bowl and refrigerate at least one hour.

Preheat oven to 450°F. In a large skillet heat olive oil, add onion and cook until onion begins to brown. Add cumin and oregano. Cook about 30 seconds. Add chilies, tomato paste, vinegar and water. Bring to a boil and reduce heat, simmer for 5 minutes. Add chicken and stir until hot.

Arrange tortilla chips on a baking sheet in a single layer. Sprinkle each chip with cheese. Spoon about 1 tablespoon of chicken mixture on top of each chip. Bake for 3 minutes or until cheese bubbles. Transfer to a serving platter. Top each chip with 1 teaspoon of Cilantro Avocado Crème. Garnish with chopped cilantro. Serve warm.

Serves 6-8

Taco Party Wings

1   package taco seasoning mix
¼   cup corn meal
¾   teaspoon salt
2   teaspoons dried parsley
2   pounds chicken wings, split

Preheat oven to 350°F. Combine dry ingredients in a plastic bag. Shake wings in bag, a few at a time, until well coated. Line a 9x12 baking dish with heavy-duty aluminum foil and spray with cooking spray. Place wings in a single layer in the pan. Bake for 30 minutes. Turn wings and bake 10 minutes more or until tender.

Serves 6-8

Sun-Dried Tomato Deviled Eggs

4   hard-boiled eggs, peeled and halved lengthwise
¼   cup chopped oil-packed, sun-dried tomatoes
¼   cup extra virgin olive oil
1   teaspoon red wine vinegar
½   clove garlic, minced
¼   teaspoon kosher salt, or to taste
    Freshly ground black pepper
4   kalamata olives, pitted and halved for garnish

Carefully remove the yolks from the whites. Mash yolks in a bowl with a fork. Blot tomatoes dry with a paper towel. Add tomatoes and the other ingredients to the yolks and blend with a fork. Stuff the yolk mixture into the whites and garnish.

Serves 4

These are a nice change from traditional deviled eggs.

Roquefort Mousse

4   ounces Roquefort cheese
4   ounces cream cheese
½   stick butter
1   clove garlic
1½   teaspoons brandy
1   cup whipping cream
¼   cup freshly squeezed lemon juice
    Fresh pear and apple slices for serving
1   can lemon-lime soda
    Pecans for garnish

Place cheeses, butter, garlic, and brandy in food processor. Process until smooth. Whip whipping cream. Fold together with cheese mixture. In a separate bowl, combine soda and lemon juice. Slice pears and apples into wedges and dip into soda and lemon juice mixture. Garnish cheese with pecans and serve with pear and apple slices.

Serves 8-12

Avocado & Jalapeño Deviled Eggs

4   hard-boiled eggs, peeled and halved lengthwise

⅓   cup mashed ripe avocado

1   tablespoon minced fresh cilantro

1   tablespoon minced green onions (white and light green parts)

1-2   teaspoons minced, seeded jalapeño pepper

1-2   teaspoons fresh lime juice

¼   teaspoon kosher salt, or to taste

   Freshly ground black pepper

   Fresh cilantro sprigs for garnish

Carefully remove the yolks from the whites. Mash in a bowl with a fork. Add the other ingredients and blend with a fork. Stuff the yolk mixture into the whites and garnish.

Serves 4

Jamie's Feta Puffs

1   sheet puff pastry dough, thawed

8   ounces basil and sun-dried tomato feta cheese

3-4   ounces cream cheese

Preheat oven to 375°F. Cut the puff pastry sheet into 36 squares. Keep dough covered with plastic wrap to prevent drying. Roll each square out until the dough is half the original thickness. Cut the feta into 36 pieces. Put 1 piece of feta and ½ teaspoon of cream cheese in the center of each square of dough. Fold the four corners of the square over the filling, so the corners overlap. Press the seams to seal. Roll each piece into a ball and place seam side down on a cookie sheet. Bake 15 minutes or until golden in color.

Serves 10-12

This recipe was inspired by caterers in San Carlos, California.

Chicken & Mushroom Quesadillas

3 teaspoons canola oil
3 boneless chicken breasts
2 tablespoons butter
3 ounces minced shallots
1 pound chopped mushrooms
2 teaspoons chili powder
1 teaspoon oregano
  Salt
  Pepper
½ cup heavy cream, heated and reduced
4 ounces bread crumbs
⅔ cup minced onions
⅓ cup chopped cilantro
2½ cups grated Monterey Jack cheese
16 small flour tortillas
  Olive oil spray

Pound chicken to even thickness. Heat sauté pan over moderately high heat and add oil. When oil is hot, add chicken breasts. Cook about 4 minutes, turn over, and continue to cook until just done, about 4 more minutes. Remove from pan, cool, and shred chicken. Set aside.

Heat butter in sauté pan. Add shallots and sauté until soft. Add mushrooms, chili powder, and oregano and cook until liquid released by the mushrooms has been reabsorbed. Season with salt and pepper, and add cream and bread crumbs. Stir to combine. Add shredded chicken, onion, and cilantro. Cool a few minutes and stir in cheese. Season with salt and pepper.

Preheat grill or oven. Spray one side of 8 tortillas with nonstick olive oil. Place tortillas oil side down on a large sheet pan. Divide chicken mixture among tortillas, spreading to even thickness. Top with remaining 8 tortillas, press, then spray with nonstick olive oil. Quesadillas may be refrigerated until ready to use (1 day) or wrap quesadillas and freeze (up to 3 months).

In an oven or frying pan, grill quesadillas until heated through and golden brown, about 3 minutes per side. Cut into wedges and serve warm with sour cream, salsa, guacamole, or other condiments as desired.

Serves 8 as appetizer, or 4 as main dish

Sausage Stars

1 pound spicy sausage
3 cups grated sharp Cheddar
    cheese
1 cup creamy ranch salad
    dressing
2¼ ounces (1 small can) ripe
    olives, drained and sliced
1 small red bell pepper, chopped
1 clove garlic, minced
1 package won ton wrappers
    (or egg roll wrappers cut in
    quarters)
    Cooking spray (butter-
    flavored is preferable, but not
    necessary)

Preheat oven to 350°F. In a frying pan, brown the sausage, then drain and dry with paper towels. In a large bowl, combine the cooked sausage with the cheese, salad dressing, olives, red bell pepper, and garlic. Spray two regular size muffin pans very lightly with cooking oil spray. Lay the won ton wrappers flat over the tops of the pans and lightly spray the top side only with cooking spray. Press the won ton wrappers into each cup to form a cup or an open star. Bake the wrappers for approximately 7 to 8 minutes, or until golden brown. Remove wrappers from the muffin pans and place on a baking sheet. Repeat this process making all the won ton wrappers.

Equally divide the sausage mixture (approximately 1 heaping teaspoon) among the baked wrappers. Bake sausage stars for 5 minutes or until bubbly. Serve warm. Stars can be made ahead, baked, and frozen. Layer on cookie sheet, freeze, then stack in freezer.

Serves 8-10

No need to thaw before reheating.

A
P
P
E
T
I
Z
E
R
S

Oven Dried Tomatoes
24 ripe Italian plum tomatoes
6-8 sprigs fresh rosemary, chopped
6-8 sprigs fresh thyme, chopped
2 tablespoons sugar

Italian Stuffed Bread

1	pound hot Italian bulk sausage
1	medium onion, chopped
4	cloves garlic, minced
2	tablespoons olive oil
1	7-ounce jar pimiento stuffed olives, drained and sliced
6	green onion tops, finely chopped
2	jalapeños, seeded and chopped
1	cup grated provolone cheese
1	cup grated mozzarella cheese
	Cooking spray
2	loaves crusty French bread refrigerator dough
8	ounces pepperoni slices
½	cup grated Parmesan cheese
½	cup Italian pesto salad dressing
1	egg, beaten

Preheat oven to 375°F. In a skillet, brown sausage in pieces, drain, and set aside. Sauté onions and garlic in a small amount of olive oil, just until wilted. Set aside. Chop sausage into small pieces.

Spray pizza stone or cookie sheet with cooking spray or grease with olive oil. Remove bread dough from can and carefully unroll, forming a rectangle about the size of the cookie sheet. Keep dough as thick as possible, do not stretch. In center third of dough, using half of ingredients, place pepperoni slices (3 per row), sausage, onion and garlic mixture, green onions and jalapeños, leaving about 1 inch of dough at each end. Divide provolone and mozzarella into 4 portions. Layer a quarter of the cheese over meat, onions, etc. Then layer half of the olives, then half of the salad dressing drizzled over mixture, then layer another quarter of the cheese.

Using a sharp knife, make cuts about 1 inch apart on each side of remaining ⅔ of dough, perpendicular to the filling. Fold strips of dough up over the mixture at an angle, alternating sides. The strips will overlap at the top of the filling. Seal dough at each end. Brush top of bread with beaten egg (to thin the egg, add a little water). Sprinkle with half of the Parmesan cheese. Prepare second loaf with remaining ingredients. Bake 15 to 20 minutes until golden. Cover top with aluminum foil if browning too quickly.

Remove to serving platter, slice into 1 to 1½ -inch servings and serve immediately. Bread can be made

A
P
P
E
T
I
Z
E
R
S

ahead and reheated before serving. Substitute different ingredients and sauces as desired.

Frozen bread dough that has been thawed may also be used. Let rise after filling, then bake, or use fresh dough.

Serves 8-10

Cheddar and Caraway Cocktail Crackers

½	cup walnuts
6	ounces sharp Cheddar cheese
1¼	cups white flour
½	teaspoon kosher salt
4	tablespoons butter, cut into pieces
1	egg yolk
2-3	tablespoons dark beer
2	tablespoons caraway seeds
2	tablespoons kosher salt

Preheat oven to 375°F. In processor bowl, fitted with blade, process the walnuts to a fine grind — be careful not to over-process into a "butter." Transfer into a side bowl and fit processor with a fine grating disk. Grate Cheddar cheese and transfer into the side bowl. Replace blade into the processor bowl and add flour, salt, and butter. Pulse processor to create a course meal. Add ground walnuts, grated cheese, and egg yolk. With processor running, add enough beer to allow a moist dough to form.

Turn dough onto a floured board and knead briefly. Form into a log, wrap in plastic, and chill for 30 minutes. Roll out dough to a thickness of ¼ inch, using a pizza cutter and a ruler, cut into 1-inch diamonds. Sprinkle caraway seeds and kosher salt over the top and press into the dough with the rolling pin. Transfer to a baking sheet and bake for 12 to 15 minutes, or until lightly browned. Transfer to wire rack until cool, then store in an airtight container.

Makes 60-80 crackers

29

APPETIZERS

Cheese Torte

1	cup sun-dried tomatoes (packed in oil)
1	bunch fresh basil
1	cup shredded Parmesan cheese
½	pound softened butter
1	pound softened cream cheese

Drain tomatoes and pulse in processor to a rough chop. Set aside. Process basil and Parmesan cheese together. Set aside. Blend together butter and cream cheese (do not over-process). Set aside. Line a 2-cup mold (any shape or style) with clear food wrap. Layer in mold as follows, (spread each layer evenly with the back of a spoon before adding the next layer): ⅓ cream cheese and butter mixture, sun-dried tomatoes, ⅓ cream cheese and butter mixture, basil and Parmesan mixture, and ⅓ cream cheese and butter mixture. Bring the food wrap over the top layer making sure it is completely covered. Refrigerate for six hours or overnight.

To serve: open the food wrap, turn over on to desired platter and lift off the mold. Peel away food wrap and smooth out any marks left from the food wrap. Serve with crackers and/or baguettes.

Serves 6-8

Cashew Butter Appetizers

2	cups toasted cashews
3	tablespoons peanut oil
	Toasted bread rounds (Melba toast)
	Mango chutney
	Bacon pieces, crisp fried

Process nuts and oil in food processor with steel blade until smooth. Spread on toasted bread rounds or Melba toast. Top with a dollop of chutney and a piece of bacon. Serve as appetizer or snack.

Serves 6-8

Smoked Oyster Spread

1	8-ounce package cream cheese
1½	tablespoons mayonnaise
1	teaspoon Worcestershire sauce
	Dash hot sauce
	Dash salt
1	tablespoon minced onion
1	3.5-ounce tin smoked oysters
	Chopped green onions
	Sweet Hungarian paprika

Combine first 5 ingredients in food processor and process until smooth. Add onion and smoked oysters. Pulse-process until desired smoothness. Chill until firm.

To serve, form chilled spread into a ball and roll in chopped green onions. Sprinkle paprika over the ball. Serve with water crackers or toast rounds.

Serves 12

The combination of the green onion and paprika garnish makes this a festive holiday appetizer.

Toasted Pecans

1	quart pecan halves
1	quart water
⅓	cup salt

Soak pecans in salt water for 1 hour. Drain well. Preheat oven to 250°F. Place pecans on large baking sheet with rim. Bake for 1 hour. Stir and test twice during toasting.

Serves 8

Delicious for snacking and attractive for gifts.

Monique's Sugared Pecans

1	egg white, unbeaten
1	cup sugar
3	tablespoons orange juice
½	teaspoon salt
¼	teaspoon cinnamon
1	teaspoon vanilla
8	cups pecans

Preheat oven to 275°F. Thoroughly mix all ingredients except pecans. Add pecans. Place on a well greased cookie sheet. Bake for 50 minutes. Makes 8 cups

Serves 16

Makes a wonderful Christmas gift!

NOTES

BEVERAGES

Contents

Lavender Lemonade

2 cups boiling water
2 tablespoons dried lavender
2 quarts lemonade less 2 cups
   water
  Sugar to taste

Place lavender in 2 cups of boiling water, steep 20 minutes, strain. Make 2 quarts of your favorite lemonade less 2 cups water. Add lemonade to strained lavender water. Serve chilled and garnish with lemon slices. Adjust to taste with more or less lavender water. Sweeten as you like.

Serves 8

Ice Ring

1 6-cup ring mold
  Assorted fresh fruit:
   Strawberries, slices of
   kiwifruit, orange, lemon, lime,
   seedless grapes, melon balls,
   mint or other herbs, edible
   flowers

Make the ice ring the day before serving the punch. Boil 7 cups of water for 1 minute. Let cool at room temperature. (This eliminates cloudiness.) Pour 3 cups of the water into ring mold and freeze. Set the remaining water aside. Arrange fruit, herbs, mint, and flowers on top of the ice in the mold. Fill the mold with remaining water to within ½ inch of the top and freeze. To unmold, let the mold sit at room temperature for 5 minutes or until loosened. Carefully float ice ring in the punch.

Makes 1 ice ring.

If you can boil water, you can make an ice ring. They are always a beautiful accent to any punch bowl. Any combination of fruit, herbs, and flowers can be put together to complement the theme of your party. Be CREATIVE!

> Cure for headaches: cut a lime in half and rub on the forehead. The throbbing will go away.

Christmas Tea

1	quart cranberry juice
1	pint orange juice
½	cup lemon juice
1	cup pineapple juice
½	cup sugar
2	cups water
4	cinnamon sticks
4	tablespoons whole clove

Bag cinnamon sticks and clove in cheesecloth. Mix all ingredients in a large pot and bring to a boil. Simmer for 15 minutes. Cool. Remove bag. Store in an airtight container in the refrigerator. Serve over ice.

Makes approximately ½ gallon.

Orange-Pineapple Smoothie

1	banana
2	cups pineapple chunks, drained
1	cup orange juice
¼	cup nonfat milk
2	tablespoons honey
4-5	ice cubes

Place all ingredients in blender and purée until smooth.

Serves 4-6

Grape Gorilla Smoothie

⅓	(5.25 ounces) of 16-ounce tub of frozen, sliced, and sweetened strawberries
¼	(3 ounces) of 11.5-ounce container of frozen grape juice concentrate
½	cup vanilla yogurt
2	ripe medium size bananas
2	teaspoons artificial sweetener or 2 tablespoons sugar (optional)
1	tray of ice cubes

Combine all ingredients and blend until smooth.

Makes 2 quarts.

After moving to Colorado from Georgia, one of our most missed treats was a grape smoothie in a local shop. This recipe has helped satisfy our craving.

Sunshine Smoothie

½   tray of frozen orange juice
    cubes
½   tray ice cubes
1   cup "yellow" fruit chunks
    (mango, peaches, and/or
    pineapple)
8   ounces container of "yellow"
    yogurt (piña colada, banana,
    or lemon; all are good.)
½   cup shredded coconut
    (optional, use if you're feeling
    "tropical")
    Dash wheat germ (optional,
    use if you're feeling
    "healthy")
1-2 cups orange juice (amount
    depends on how slushy you
    want the smoothie to be)

Place all ingredients in a blender and
blend until smooth.

Serves 1

Frozen Passion

2   14-ounce cans condensed milk
1   2-liter bottle or five 12-ounce
    cans carbonated lemon lime
    soda

Mix all ingredients together and put
in ice cream freezer.

Makes 2-3 quarts.

*Frozen Passion is like sherbet.
It's a great summer treat for
children. For adults, rum can be
added to this drink.*

Light Café Frappé

2   tablespoons instant coffee
¾   cup warm water
1   14-ounce can fat-free
    sweetened condensed milk
1   teaspoon vanilla extract
4   cups ice cubes

In small bowl, dissolve coffee in
water. In blender container, combine
dissolved coffee, condensed milk, and
vanilla. Blend well. Gradually add ice,
blending until smooth.

Serves 4

*You can indulge your taste buds
without indulging your hips!*

East India Cocktail

1½ ounces Cognac
½ ounce Curacao or Triple Sec
1 ounce pineapple juice
  Dash of Angostura Bitters

Measure ingredients into a cocktail shaker and shake over ice. This can be served over ice, or additional pineapple juice can be added to dilute it. Serve in lowball glasses.

Serves 2

India does not have a lot in the way of their own signature cocktails, instead preferring to draw upon their European influences. This cocktail at least has an appropriate name, although it is not known for sure how authentic it is to India.

Mardi Gras Mary

1 32-ounce bottle Bloody Mary mix
¾ cup Vodka
1 teaspoon steak sauce (or more to taste)
  Lemon slices, celery sticks, or spicy beans for garnish

Combine all ingredients in a large shaker or pitcher with lots of ice. Shake or stir well and pour over ice in tall glasses. Garnish.

Serves 8

Meme's Martini

1¾ cups pomegranate juice
2 ounces Absolute Citron vodka
1 ounce Cointreau
  Lemon slice
  Pomegranate fruit (optional)

Put pomegranate juice, vodka, and Cointreau in a shaker with ice. Shake well. Pour into two chilled martini glasses. Garnish with pomegranate fruit and add a squeeze of lemon.

Serves 2

Sex on the Beach

2	parts Midori
1	part vodka
1	part raspberry liqueur
2	parts pineapple juice
2	parts cranberry juice

Combine all ingredients in a large shaker or pitcher with lots of ice. Shake or stir well and pour over ice. Serve.

Can make enough for one or a crowd.

White Sangría

⅓	cup lime juice
⅓	cup orange juice
⅔	cup sugar
1	cup sparkling water, divided
3	cups white wine
¼	cup tequila

Mix lime juice, orange juice, sugar, and ¼ cup sparkling water. Stir until sugar dissolves. Add wine, remaining water, and tequila.

Exact amounts are not necessary. You can use less sugar and substitute juices in an emergency. For a crowd, make two batches, one with white wine and one with red wine for the traditionalists.

Serves 6-8

Champagne Punch

1	20-ounce can crushed pineapple in heavy syrup
1	cup fresh lemon juice
1	cup maraschino cherry juice
1	cup dark rum
½	cup brandy
1	bottle (750 ml) brut champagne, chilled

In a large punch bowl or pitcher, stir pineapple, lemon juice, cherry juice, rum, and brandy to blend. Chill for at least 30 minutes. Add any kind of brut champagne just before serving.

Serves 8

Triple Candy Cane

1 part peppermint schnapps
1 part half-and-half
Ice
Peppermint candies, crushed

Combine the schnapps and half-and-half in roughly equal quantities. Add ice and crushed peppermint candies, blend, and serve.

Can make enough for one or a crowd.

This is a fun, easy holiday drink and it's easy to make as much or little as you need.

Après Chocolate

1 ½ ounces Kahlúa
½ ounce Cointreau
¼ ounce Godiva Dark Chocolate Liqueur
1 ¼ cups steamed milk
Whipped cream
Ground cinnamon for garnish

Combine alcohol in a warmed coffee mug and add milk. Stir and add a dollop of whipped cream on top. Garnish with a sprinkle of cinnamon, or add a cinnamon stick stirrer.

Serves 1

This is perfect for after-ski relaxing, but don't plan on driving!

Hot Buttered Rum Mix

1 cup butter, softened
1 cup packed brown sugar
½ cup powdered sugar
1 teaspoon ground nutmeg
1 teaspoon ground cinnamon
2 cups vanilla ice cream, softened
Rum
Boiling water

In a small bowl, beat together butter, brown sugar, powdered sugar, nutmeg, and cinnamon until well combined. Beat in softened ice cream. Place mixture in freezer container, seal, and freeze. Makes about 4 cups of mix. For one serving, spoon about ⅓ cup frozen mixture into a mug, add 1 jigger of rum, and ½ cup boiling water. Stir well.

Serves 12

Hot Cajun Eggnog

3   12-ounce cans evaporated milk
2   cups milk
4   egg yolks
1   cup sugar
¼   teaspoon salt
4   egg whites
3   tablespoons sugar
    Nutmeg, freshly grated
    Bourbon, 1 tablespoon per serving

In a saucepan, scald milk, and then remove from heat. In a separate bowl, beat egg yolks and one cup of sugar until fluffy. Add salt and a little scalded milk to the egg mixture, being careful not to let eggs cook. Continue adding milk in small portions until about half of the milk is incorporated. Pour egg mixture into remaining milk and stir constantly. Turn stove to medium heat and cook mixture, stirring constantly, until it thickens. Remove from heat. In a separate bowl, beat egg whites with 3 tablespoons sugar and then fold into hot milk. Sprinkle with fresh grated nutmeg. Add bourbon to taste for each serving. May be served warm or cold.

Serves 6-8

Homemade Kahlúa

6   cups water
5   cups sugar
4   cups water
2   ounces instant coffee, not freeze-dried
2   ounces vanilla
1   pint grain alcohol

Boil 6 cups water with sugar until sugar is dissolved. In separate pan, gently boil 4 cups of water with coffee for 5 minutes. Let both pans cool completely. Put in freezer. When completely cold, add alcohol and vanilla. Stir well. Pour into liquor bottles or decanters and let sit a few weeks before opening. Makes great drinks or can be used in Tiramisu.

Makes 3 quarts

Cool liquid mixtures in freezer.

Limoncello/Lemon Liqueur

12	medium lemons
2	cups granulated sugar
1	liter grain alcohol (vodka also works fine)
2	cups water

If possible, start with organic lemons or at least non-wax, coated lemons. Wash lemons well, then zest and place zest in a 2-quart glass container with tight-fitting lid. Cover the zest with the alcohol and seal the container. Set aside in a dark, cool place for one week. After the week, create simple syrup by combining water and sugar in a saucepan. Put pan on moderate heat and stir frequently until the sugar dissolves and the mixture boils. Remove from heat and cool to room temperature. When cool, add syrup to lemon/alcohol mix. Set aside for another week.

After week two, strain mixture through funnel lined with a double layer of cheesecloth into clean glass bottles. (You can use old wine bottles or funky liter-sized soda bottles.) Store in the freezer. It won't freeze but it will become thick and yummy. Serve as you would an apéritif in small glasses before or after dinner. Also, if you're having a gin and tonic but don't have any limes, a shot of Limoncello usually does the trick.

Limoncello, also known as "electric lemonade" is a wonderful treat to make for Christmas gifts. Just multiply the recipe accordingly. Zesting lemons gets old fast! Invite a bunch of friends to bring their own cheese graters and make a party out of it. Have some of the previous batch of Limoncello on hand for incentive.

Freeze leftover wine in ice cube trays
for future use in casseroles and sauces.

SALADS

Contents

Indonesian Rice Salad

| 2 | cups brown rice |
| 3 | cups water |

Bring water to a boil, add rice. Reduce to simmer, cover, and cook until tender, approximately 35-45 minutes.

DRESSING

⅓	cup peanut oil
3	tablespoons sesame oil
½	cup orange juice
1-2	cloves garlic, minced
1	teaspoon salt
2	tablespoons soy sauce
½	teaspoon crushed red pepper
2	tablespoons rice vinegar or cider vinegar
1	cup crushed pineapple

SALAD

3	scallions, minced
1	celery stalk, minced
1	medium red or green bell pepper, diced
1	8-ounce can water chestnuts, drained
½	pound bean sprouts
½	cup raisins
1	cup peanuts, chopped
2	tablespoons sesame seeds
1	cup cubed firm tofu (optional)

In a medium sized bowl, combine all dressing ingredients. Add hot rice and mix well. Cool to room temperature, cover and refrigerate. Before serving, add salad ingredients. Mix well.

Serves 4-6

This is a wonderful salad with no altitude attention required (other than that rice may take longer to get tender) and has been quite popular at potlucks, and summer parties.

Orzo Salad

¾	cup orzo, cooked according to package instructions
⅓	cup minced oil-packed sun-dried tomatoes
4	tablespoons olive oil
4	tablespoons balsamic vinegar
¼	cup sliced Kalamata olives
1	cup chopped onion
1	garlic clove, minced
½	cup minced fresh basil
½	cup toasted pine nuts
½	cup grated Parmesan cheese

In a medium-sized bowl, add tomatoes, oil, vinegar, and olives to hot orzo and toss. Let stand to cool. Add remaining ingredients when ready to serve. Best served at room temperature.

Serves 8

Crunchy Chinese Salad

SALAD
2 packages Top Ramen Chicken Sesame Noodles
2 tablespoons butter
½ cup sesame or sunflower seeds
½ cup slivered almonds
1½ heads Chinese cabbage
4-5 green onions

DRESSING
½ cup corn oil
¼ cup red wine vinegar
½ cup sugar
1 teaspoon soy sauce

Crumble the noodles in a bowl. Save the sesame oil packet and discard the seasoning packet. In a 12-inch frying pan, heat the butter over medium heat and brown the noodles. Add seeds and almonds, brown. Add the sesame oil packet from the noodles (watch carefully because it burns easily). Cool.

Cut off end of Chinese cabbage. Slice lengthwise into quarters. Chop into ¼-½-inch strips. Slice green onion tops crosswise approximately ¼-½-inch wide. Discard root end. Toss noodle mixture with cabbage mixture just before serving. Noodles will become soggy if mixed ahead.

Measure oil, vinegar, sugar and soy sauce into a wide mouth bottle with secure top. Shake well to blend. Shake dressing, pour over salad.

Serves 10-12

Black sesame seeds add nice color to this salad.

Rice and Artichoke Salad

1 package chicken flavored rice mix
4 green onions, thinly sliced
½ green bell pepper, diced
12 pimiento stuffed olives, sliced
2 6-ounce jars marinated artichoke hearts
¾ teaspoon curry powder
⅓ cup mayonnaise

Cook rice as directed, omitting butter. Cool in a large bowl. Add onions, green pepper and olives. Drain the artichoke hearts, reserving marinade, and halve. In a small bowl, make the dressing by combining artichoke marinade with curry powder and mayonnaise. Add artichoke hearts to rice salad and toss with dressing. Chill.

Serves 8-10

Great summer salad!

Primavera Pasta Salad

SALAD

1	medium zucchini, diced
1	medium green bell pepper, diced
1	medium red bell pepper, diced
½	cup chopped fresh parsley
1	large tomato, diced (or substitute 1 15-ounce can diced tomatoes)
1	medium red onion, diced
1	small can jumbo black olives, sliced
3	ounces pepperoni or salami, cut into small pieces
4	ounces Provolone cheese, cubed
8-10	ounces spinach fettuccine
¼	cup extra virgin olive oil

VINAIGRETTE

1-2	large cloves garlic
¼	cup salad oil
2	tablespoons extra virgin olive oil
½	teaspoon dried oregano
2	tablespoons red wine vinegar
2	tablespoons fresh basil
½	teaspoon salt
	Coarsely ground black pepper

Cook fettuccine al dente, rinse with cold water, drain, and place in mixing bowl. Toss with a couple drops of olive oil. Set aside.

Dice zucchini, peppers, tomato and onion. Chop parsley. Add these to the pasta along with the black olives. Cut pepperoni or salami into small pieces and add meat and cheese to salad.

Chop garlic in food processor, add all other ingredients in order and process briefly. Pour vinaigrette dressing over salad and toss.

Serves 8 to 12 entrée servings

Make this salad several hours ahead of time to allow the flavors to blend. Serve at room temperature.

**S
A
L
A
D
S**

**Do not use metal bowls when mixing salads.
Use wooden, glass or china.**

Lobster Cobb Salad

SALAD

2   ripe avocados, peeled, pitted, cut in ¾-inch cubes

Juice of 1 lemon

1½   pounds cooked lobster meat, cut in ¾-inch cubes

1   pint cherry tomatoes, halved or quartered

1½   teaspoons salt

½   teaspoon freshly ground black pepper

½   pound lean bacon, cooked and crumbled

¾   cup crumbled blue cheese

1   bunch arugula, washed and spun dry

VINAIGRETTE

1½   tablespoons Dijon mustard

1⅓   cups freshly squeezed lemon juice

5   tablespoons olive oil

¾   teaspoon salt

½   teaspoon freshly ground black pepper

Toss the avocado with the lemon juice. If the arugula leaves are large, cut them in half. Put the lobster and tomatoes in a bowl. Sprinkle with salt and pepper and toss with enough vinaigrette to moisten. Add the avocados, bacon, cheese and arugula and toss again. Serve at room temperature.

To make the vinaigrette, in a small bowl, whisk ingredients together and let sit.

Serves 6

You can get lobster meat from many gourmet markets pre-cooked and shelled/picked, which saves some trouble.

This is an absolutely gorgeous salad, with lots of color. The only thing you might consider changing is the dressing. The vinaigrette above is very good, but it's in stark contrast to the buttery taste of the lobster. If you're looking for a creamier taste you might want to consider bleu cheese or other salad dressing.

S
A
L
A
D
S

If produce is unripe when purchased, put vegetables or fruits such as avocados, bananas, or peaches in a brown paper bag in a dark cupboard to ripen more quickly.

Omega-3 Salad

2　tablespoons walnut
　　or canola oil
2　tablespoons white wine vinegar
2　small cloves garlic, minced
¼　teaspoon salt, or to taste
　　Freshly ground black pepper,
　　　to taste
½　cup finely chopped celery
1　pound fresh, wild salmon fillet,
　　　grilled, or 1 15-ounce can
　　　pink or red Alaskan (wild)
　　　salmon, backbone and skin
　　　removed
¼　cup light canola mayonnaise or
　　　other low fat mayonnaise
1　tablespoon freshly squeezed
　　　lemon juice
　　Salt and pepper to taste
4　cups baby spinach leaves
8　cherry tomatoes, cut in half
¼　cup finely chopped walnuts

In a small bowl, whisk together oil, vinegar, garlic, salt and pepper for dressing and set aside. Mix celery with salmon and toss with mayonnaise and lemon juice. Season to taste with salt and pepper. In large bowl, toss spinach with dressing. Top with salmon mixture. Place cherry tomato halves around platter. Sprinkle with walnuts.

Serves 4

49

Mexican Chopped Salad

SALAD

4　cups packed chopped romaine
　　　lettuce
1　Hass avocado, pitted, peeled
　　　and cut in ½-inch cubes
½　cup canned corn, drained
2　hard-boiled eggs, chopped
1　plum tomato, diced
¼　cup chopped red onion

DRESSING

2　tablespoons canola oil
1　tablespoon fresh lime juice
½　teaspoon ground cumin
½　teaspoon salt

In large bowl combine dressing ingredients and whisk together. Add romaine, avocado, and corn; toss to coat. Arrange salad on a large platter and top with eggs, tomato, and red onion.

Serves 4

Mayan Salad

SALAD

2	quarts crisp greens, torn into bite-size pieces
1½	cups jicama (cut in juilenne strips) or sliced water chestnuts
1	medium-size mild red onion, sliced
1	grapefruit
2	oranges
½	pound cherry tomatoes, halved
1	large avocado

CUMIN DRESSING

3	tablespoons cider vinegar
2	tablespoons fresh lime juice
6	tablespoons olive oil or salad oil
1	clove garlic
1	teaspoon black pepper
½	teaspoon salt
½	teaspoon ground cumin
⅛	teaspoon crushed red pepper

Mix greens and jicama in large salad bowl, arrange onion rings on top. Peel grapefruit and oranges, remove all seeds and white membrane from sections, and arrange sections atop onions along with tomatoes. Cover: chill 1 to 2 hours. Blend dressing ingredients well, set aside.

To serve, peel, pit and slice avocado; arrange on salad. Dress and mix gently.

Serves 6 to 8

Spicy Mexican main dishes benefit from a crunchy, cooling salad companion. For greens, use iceberg or butter lettuce, romaine, or spinach; or present a combination of two or three.

S
A
L
A
D
S

Spinach Salad with Warm Dressing

4	slices bacon
1	bunch fresh spinach
¼	red onion, chopped
3	tomatoes, seeded and chopped
½	cup fresh mushrooms, sliced
2	eggs, hard cooked and sliced
½	cup feta cheese crumbles
1	tablespoon Dijon mustard
1	tablespoon honey
2	tablespoons Italian salad dressing
	Salt and pepper
	Croutons

Cook bacon until crisp, drain and crumble; reserve drippings; set aside. Wash and remove stems from spinach, tear leaves into bite-size pieces. Drain well. Place spinach in large bowl. Add onion, tomatoes, mushrooms, bacon pieces, sliced eggs, and cheese. Toss well.

Put 1 tablespoon bacon drippings, Dijon mustard, honey, and salad dressing in glass measuring cup or small bowl; heat in microwave until warm. Stir and drizzle over salad. Season with salt and pepper. Mix slightly. Add croutons and serve immediately.

Serves 4

Mediterranean Vegetable and Egg Salad

Salad

1   14-ounce can artichoke hearts, drained and quartered

1   cup cherry or grape tomatoes, halved

½   cup Kalamata olives, pitted and halved

1   tablespoon capers

1   tablespoon minced red onion

2   tablespoons chopped fresh parsley

2   heads Bibb lettuce, separated into leaves

6   large hard-boiled eggs, quartered

Dressing

2   tablespoons red wine vinegar

1   teaspoon Dijon mustard

¼   teaspoon salt

¼   teaspoon pepper

⅓   cup extra virgin olive oil

Combine artichoke hearts, tomatoes, olives, capers, onion and parsley in a large bowl, add 2 tablespoons of the dressing and toss to coat. Place lettuce in a serving bowl, top with artichoke mixture and eggs. Drizzle with remaining dressing and serve.

Combine vinegar, mustard, salt and pepper in a jar with a tight-fitting lid, shake once, add oil and shake vigorously to mix.

Serves 4

51

Fresh Corn Salad

6   ears corn

3   large tomatoes, diced

1   large onion, diced

¼   cup chopped fresh basil

2   tablespoons white vinegar
     Salt and pepper to taste

Place corn in boiling water for 7-10 minutes. Cut kernels off cob. Toss all ingredients. Chill until ready to serve.

Serves 6-8

Cucumber-Mint Raita

- 2 cups whole-milk yogurt
- 1 large unpeeled English cucumber, quartered, seeded and coarsely grated
- 1 medium tomato, seeded and chopped
- ¼ cup (packed) chopped fresh mint leaves
- 1 teaspoon ground cumin
- ¼ teaspoon cayenne pepper
- ½ teaspoon salt
- ¼ teaspoon black pepper

Line a colander with a layer of paper towels and place over a plate. Spoon the yogurt into the colander on top of the paper towels and allow this to drain for about 20-30 minutes. Discard any collected liquid. Wrap grated cucumber in paper towels and squeeze out as much moisture as possible.

Whisk yogurt, mint, cumin, and cayenne pepper in a mixing bowl to blend. Add cucumbers, tomatoes, salt and pepper and stir to combine. Cover and refrigerate at least two hours.

Serves 4-6

Include about ¼ cup on the plate with the entrée.

This can be prepared up to one day in advance.

Cumin Coleslaw

- 2 tablespoons mayonnaise
- 1 tablespoon sour cream
- 1 jalapeño pepper, seeded and minced
- 1 tablespoon chopped cilantro
- ½ teaspoon cumin
  Salt and pepper
- ¼ small cabbage, thinly sliced
- 1 carrot, shredded
- 1 green onion, thinly sliced

Combine mayonnaise, sour cream, jalapeño pepper, cilantro, and cumin, season with salt and pepper. Add cabbage, carrot, and green onion. Toss to mix well. Refrigerate until serving time.

Serves 2

Spinach, White Bean, and Bacon Salad with Maple-Mustard Dressing

SALAD

1	15.5-ounce can Great Northern beans, rinsed and drained
½	cup thinly sliced green onions
½	cup finely chopped red bell pepper
3	bacon slices, cooked and crumbled
2	7-ounce packages of fresh baby spinach

DRESSING

¼	cup maple syrup
3	tablespoons apple cider vinegar
1	tablespoon extra virgin olive oil
1	tablespoon Dijon mustard
¼	teaspoon salt
¼	teaspoon freshly ground black pepper

In a microwave-safe bowl, combine dressing ingredients stirring with a whisk. Microwave on HIGH 1 minute or until hot. Place beans in a glass bowl and microwave on HIGH 1 minute or until hot.

Combine onions, bell peppers, bacon, and spinach in a large bowl. Add syrup mixture and beans, toss well. Serve immediately.

Serves 8

Green Salad Plus

SALAD

5	cups torn romaine lettuce
2	medium tomatoes, cut into wedges
¾	cup shredded Swiss cheese
⅓	cup shredded Parmesan cheese
1	cup seasoned salad croutons
1	cup slivered almonds, toasted
4	bacon strips, cooked and crumbled

DRESSING

¾	cup vegetable oil
2	tablespoons lemon juice
3	garlic gloves, minced
¼	teaspoon salt
	Dash of pepper

In a jar with a tight-fitting lid, combine the oil, lemon juice, garlic, salt and pepper. Shake well. In a large bowl, combine the lettuce, tomatoes and cheeses. Drizzle with dressing and toss to coat. Sprinkle with the croutons, almonds and bacon.

Serves: 6

This is a good choice when a run of the mill salad isn't special enough. Cook a pound of bacon at a time and keep it in the freezer. With the added convenience of shredded cheese and packaged salad greens, there isn't much preparation time required.

Curly Endive and Bacon Salad with Mustard Anchovy Dressing

SALAD

1	pound thick sliced bacon cut into ½-inch pieces
⅓	cup olive oil
3	garlic cloves, lightly crushed
6	cups French bread, trimmed and ¾-inch cubed
2	heads curly endive, torn into bite size pieces

DRESSING

3	tablespoons Dijon mustard
3	tablespoons fresh lemon juice
1½	tablespoons anchovy paste
1	teaspoon pepper
1	cup olive oil
	Salt

Cook bacon in heavy skillet over medium heat until crisp and brown. Using slotted spoon, transfer bacon to paper towels and drain. Pour off all but 2 tablespoons fat from skillet. Add ⅓ cup oil and garlic to same skillet and cook over medium heat until garlic is golden, stirring frequently, about 5 minutes. Discard the garlic from the skillet using a slotted spoon. Add bread to skillet and toss to coat in oil mixture. Cook until crisp and golden, stirring frequently, about 10 minutes. Transfer croutons to a large bowl. Add the endive and bacon. Toss with enough dressing to season to taste. Divide salad among plates to serve.

Whisk first 4 dressing ingredients in small bowl. Gradually whisk in oil. Season to taste with salt, cover, and refrigerate. Bring to room temperature before using.

Serves 8

Serve this salad between the main course and dessert.

If you don't like endive, feel free to substitute baby spinach or arugula. Dressing can be prepared 1 day ahead.

If lettuce starts turning a little brown (but not slimy), it may not be suitable for salads, but is fine for sautéing. Sautéed salad greens like lettuce, radicchio, and endive make an unusual but tasty side dish. Sauté just like spinach. Cook quickly in a little olive oil, minced garlic, and salt.

54

S
A
L
A
D
S

Green Bean, Cucumber and Feta Salad

½	cup olive oil
⅛	cup white wine vinegar
1½	tablespoons lemon juice
¼	teaspoon paprika
¼	teaspoon dry mustard
1½	teaspoons dill weed
2	16-ounce cans green beans (cut or whole), drained
	Salt and pepper to taste
½	cup mayonnaise
5	tablespoons sour cream
¼	cup blue cheese
1½-2	bunches green onions, chopped
2	cucumbers, sliced

Mix olive oil, vinegar, lemon juice, paprika, mustard, dill weed, salt and pepper. Add the mayonnaise, sour cream and bleu cheese to the mixture. Pour over beans and marinate for at least two hours before serving. Add green onions and cucumbers and toss lightly.

Serves 6-8

A fantastic different salad.

May be prepared a day in advance.

Asparagus Strawberry Salad

SALAD

1	pound asparagus
	Juice from ½ lemon
½	teaspoon sugar
½	pound strawberries
1	large head of radicchio
3	ounces Prosciutto ham

DRESSING

4	ounces balsamic vinegar
2	ounces walnut oil
½	bunch of fresh parsley, finely chopped
	Salt, white pepper

Wash the asparagus and break off the ends, cut into bite size pieces; add the lemon juice, sugar and salt to boiling water and blanch the asparagus. Drain and set aside. Wash the strawberries and cut them in half. Wash the Radicchio and break into pieces. Separate Prosciutto into strips and finely chop the parsley.

Mix the vinegar, salt and pepper with the oil and add the parsley.

Mix the asparagus, strawberries, radicchio and ham together. Add the vinaigrette and toss.

Serves 6

Broccoli, Cranberry and Pecan Salad

½ cup mayonnaise

2 tablespoons sugar

2 teaspoons white or cider vinegar

¼ cup thinly sliced red onion

½ cup dried cranberries

1 14.5-ounce can mandarin orange segments

¼ cup sugared pecans (optional)

4 cups broccoli florets (1 bunch)

3-4 slices bacon, cooked and crumbled

In a small bowl, mix mayonnaise, sugar and vinegar. In a large bowl, toss broccoli, onion and bacon. Stir in the mayonnaise mixture. Add cranberries, mandarin oranges, and pecans.

Serves 4

S
A
L
A
D
S

Raspberry Walnut Salad

SALAD

1 head Boston lettuce, leaves separated

¼ cup finely chopped red onion

½ cup chopped walnuts

½ cup feta cheese

1 cup sliced mushrooms

¾ cups dried cranberries

DRESSING

½ cup canola oil

¼ cup raspberry vinegar or apple cider vinegar

2 tablespoons sugar or one packet artificial sweetener

½ teaspoon salt

½ teaspoon dry mustard

1 green onion, finely chopped

Layer the salad ingredients, in order, on a serving platter. In a jar with a tight-fitting lid, add all dressing ingredients, shake vigorously to mix. Shake the dressing mixture just before serving and pour on salad.

Serves 4

This salad is dramatic served on a platter or in a glass bowl.

Summer Fruit Salad

2 ripe peaches, peeled, pitted and sliced
1 pint fresh blueberries
1-2 cups green grapes, halved
1 pint fresh strawberries, halved or sliced
1 pint heavy whipping cream
6 tablespoons sugar
1 8-ounce cream cheese
1 teaspoon vanilla extract
   Macadamia nuts, chopped

In a clear glass serving bowl, layer half of the peaches. Layer on all the blueberries, then grapes, ending with a layer of strawberries. In a separate bowl, beat the whipping cream until stiff peaks form. Add softened cream cheese and vanilla. Beat until creamy. Small lumps may remain. Smooth the topping over the strawberries. Place a ring of remaining sliced peaches around the edge of the cream and fill the center with nuts.

Serves 10-12

This is a beautiful dish which can be served as a salad or dessert.

Taffy Apple Salad

4 cups cored and diced apples
1 8-ounce can chunk pineapple, drain and reserve juice
1 9-ounce frozen non-dairy whipped topping
1 egg, beaten
1 tablespoon flour
½ cup sugar
2 tablespoons cider vinegar
   Salted peanuts (NOT dry roast)

Mix flour, sugar, pineapple juice, egg and vinegar in medium saucepan. Stir continuously over low heat until thick. Refrigerate in pan for 2-3 hours or overnight, when sauce is cold, fold in non-dairy topping. Add apples, pineapple and peanuts. Garnish with some chopped peanuts sprinkled on top.

Serves 6-8

This can be served as a side dish or as a dessert.

Buttermilk Blue Cheese Dressing

1   large egg
2   cloves garlic, minced
1   cup vegetable or olive oil
¼   cup buttermilk
¼   teaspoon salt, or more to taste
¼   teaspoon black pepper
¼   teaspoon cayenne pepper
1   cup crumbled blue cheese
1   green onion, chopped

In a food processor, blend egg and garlic until smooth, add oil slowly in a stream. Add buttermilk, salt and peppers and process until smooth. Transfer to bowl and stir in bleu cheese and green onion. Chill for at least 2 hours, or preferably overnight.

Makes 2 cups

58

**S
A
L
A
D
S**

Creamy Lemon Vinaigrette

½   large egg yolk
2   tablespoons fresh lemon juice
½   cup extra-virgin olive oil
2   tablespoons heavy cream
     Salt
     Black pepper, freshly ground

In a small bowl, whisk the egg yolk with the lemon juice. Whisk in the olive oil and cream. Season with salt and pepper. Serve immediately.

Makes ½ cup

Serve with lettuce and crudités.

Creole Salad Dressing

1   egg
3   tablespoons Creole mustard
1   teaspoon salt
1   teaspoon black pepper
1   teaspoon hot pepper sauce
3   tablespoons Worcestershire sauce
1   teaspoon minced garlic
4   tablespoons grated Parmesan cheese
2   teaspoons prepared horseradish
⅓   cup dark vinegar
1   cup olive oil

Combine all ingredients in mixing bowl, except olive oil. Whip until thoroughly mixed. Pour olive oil in slowly, while whipping vigorously.

Makes 2 cups

Garlic Salad Dressing

4   large cloves garlic, quartered
1   heaping tablespoon salt
1   teaspoon fresh ground black pepper
3   ounces garlic red wine vinegar
12   ounces safflower oil

Put in bottle and let sit a few hours. Refrigerate, shake before serving.

Makes 1 pint

The secret to this is a heaping tablespoon of salt. No one wants to use that much, and they usually don't, then say, "Mine didn't taste like yours at all". So, when I say heaping, I really mean it!

Mango Vinaigrette Dressing

1   ripe mango, peeled, pitted and sliced
     Juice of 1 lime
½   cup vegetable oil
¼   cup rum (optional)
1   scallion, chopped
½   green bell pepper, chopped
1   inch-long piece of fresh ginger, peeled and chopped
½   teaspoon ground black pepper

Blend the mango slices with the lime juice and oil. Add the remaining ingredients. Pour over any salad of fresh vegetables. Chill before serving.

Makes 1 cup

¼ cup of rum is a bit strong for me, I usually cut it down by half.

Seedy Salad Dressing

1   cup vegetable oil
½   cup sugar
⅓   cup balsamic vinegar
1   teaspoon dried onion flakes
1   teaspoon dry mustard
1   teaspoon salt
1   teaspoon poppy seeds
1   teaspoon sesame seeds

Mix together in 2 cup container. Serve or save refrigerated.

Makes about 2 cups

Sherry Vinaigrette Dressing

¼   cup extra virgin olive oil, divided

2   shallots, minced

2   cloves garlic, minced

½   cup sherry vinegar, divided

½   cup nonfat low-sodium chicken or vegetable broth

⅛   teaspoon ground red pepper

2   teaspoons salt (preferably kosher)

¼   teaspoon freshly ground black pepper

In a medium-size nonstick skillet, heat 1 tablespoon olive oil. Add shallots and garlic, and sauté 2 minutes or until shallots are translucent and garlic is fragrant. Add ¼ cup vinegar and boil until reduced by half. Add broth and boil 2 minutes. Stir in remaining oil and vinegar, red pepper, salt and black pepper. Pour into 2 cup container. Serve or save refrigerated.

Makes about 1 cup

S
A
L
A
D
S

Basic Balsamic Vinaigrette

3   parts extra virgin olive oil

1   part balsamic vinegar

Fresh garlic, pressed

Oregano, 1 teaspoon dried or 1 tablespoon fresh

Basil, 1 teaspoon dried or 1 tablespoon fresh

Salt

Black pepper

In a salad bowl or a jar, add garlic and salt to taste and press into bottom of bowl with a spoon or shake well in a jar. (Your vinaigrette will have a fuller garlic flavor if you use salad bowl technique, although there's a lot to be said for the jar method when needing large quantities of vinaigrette.) Add vinegar, oregano, basil and fresh ground pepper, stir or shake until emulsified.

Can be made for one or to serve a crowd.

Memorize this recipe so you can use it in an amazing variety of recipes: to marinate artichoke hearts or mushrooms, to simply toss with crisp salad greens, to toss with steamed beets or to serve as a marinade for fresh tuna steaks.

Add a scant teaspoon Dijon mustard, use chopped scallions instead of garlic, use shallots instead of garlic.

SOUPS

Contents

Gumbo Z'Herbes, Green Gumbo or Wet Pot

1   pound andouille, chorizo, or other spicy smoked pork sausage

½   pound baked ham, cut into ½-inch cubes

1   cup chopped onions

1   cup water

½   cup vegetable or olive oil

8   large bags of spinach, stemmed, washed, and drained

⅛   teaspoon cayenne pepper (optional)

     Salt to taste

¼   teaspoon freshly ground black pepper

2   whole bay leaves, crushed

½   teaspoon dried thyme

½   teaspoon dried marjoram

2   whole cloves

5   whole allspice berries

8-12 cups cooked rice

In a large heavy pot, cook sausage, ham, and onions in oil on medium heat, stirring thoroughly. Continue browning for 5 minutes. Remove from pot and set aside. Pour 1 cup of water and scrape drippings from the bottom of the pot. Add half the spinach, cover, and simmer for 10 minutes. Add remaining spinach and more water if needed. Simmer for 12-15 minutes. Stir in the meat mixture and remaining seasonings. Salt to taste. Add water to cover the mixture. Raise the heat to high and bring gumbo to a boil. Reduce heat to low and simmer for 1½ hours. Serve over cooked rice.

Serves 8

Gumbo Z'herbes, also known as "Wet Pot," is neither okra nor filé gumbo, and originally it contained no meat, seafood, or game. It was a Lenten dish and traditionally served on Good Friday. No longer exclusively a Lenten dish, Gumbo Z'Herbes is often prepared with meat, sausage, seafood, or whatever the Cajuns happen to have on hand. Legend had it that you would make as many friends as the number of different greens you put in the gumbo. Other greens that are wonderful in this dish are collard greens, mustard greens, turnip greens, green cabbage, beet tops, radish tops, and watercress.

SOUPS

Crock Pot Lamb Stew

1	pound lamb, (beef or pork may be substituted) cut into bite-size cubes
2	tablespoons vegetable oil
4	cups beef broth
1	cup dry red wine
2	cloves garlic, minced
1	teaspoon crushed dried marjoram
1	bay leaf
2	cups potatoes, peeled and cubed
	Salt and pepper to taste
1½	cups sliced celery
½	cup chopped onion
1½	cups sliced carrots
½	cup sour cream
2	tablespoons flour

In a skillet, heat oil. Brown meat in hot oil, drain fat, and put meat in crock pot. Add broth, wine, garlic, marjoram, bay leaf, potatoes, salt, and pepper. Simmer at least 3-4 hours. Stir in remaining vegetables and simmer another 1-2 hours until meat and vegetables are tender. Add another 1-2 cups of water or broth while cooking if needed. Discard bay leaf. Mix sour cream and flour and stir ½ cup of the stew liquid into the mixture. Return mixture to pot and stir well.

Serves 6-8

Meal-in-Itself Minestrone

1	pound beef stew meat, cut into bite-sized pieces
5	cups water
1	onion, chopped
1	clove garlic, minced
1	14.5-ounce can peeled whole tomatoes
2	8-ounce cans tomato sauce
1	teaspoon seasoned salt
1	teaspoon basil leaves
1	teaspoon marjoram leaves
	Pepper to taste
2	carrots, sliced into 1-inch rounds
1	zucchini, sliced
¼	head cabbage, shredded
1	15.5-ounce can small red beans
1½	cups cooked corkscrew macaroni
	Parmesan cheese

In a 4-quart (or larger) slow cooker, combine beef, water, onion, garlic, tomatoes, tomato sauce, herbs, and seasonings. Cook on low 9-10 hours. Add vegetables and beans. Cook on high for 1 hour. Just before serving, stir in cooked macaroni. Garnish with Parmesan cheese.

Serves 10

Swiss Chard, Cannellini Bean, and Barley Soup

1	pound Swiss chard
¼	cup extra virgin olive oil
1	cup finely chopped onion
½	cup finely chopped celery
½	cup finely chopped carrot
⅓	cup canned, diced tomatoes, with juice
	Salt and freshly ground black pepper
4	cans chicken stock or water (8 cups)
½	cup pearl barley
2	15-ounce cans cannellini beans, drained and rinsed
	Grated Parmesan cheese

Soak chard in cold water and wash completely in several changes of cold water. Cut leaves off stalks and cut leaves into narrow strips about ¼-inch wide. Cut stalks into ⅛-inch strips. Wilt onion in the olive oil in a soup pot and cook onion until light gold. Add celery and carrots. Cook for 6 or 7 more minutes. Add tomatoes, stirring once or twice. Add chard and mix well. Cover pot and turn heat to lowest setting and simmer until chard is done. Cook barley in water or stock according to directions on package. Mix barley, cooking liquid, and rinsed beans with chard and other vegetables in soup pot. Add salt and pepper to taste and bring to a boil. Serve with grated Parmesan.

Serves 8

Assyrian Beef Stew

3	pounds of beef stew meat or beef shanks
1	large onion, chopped or 1 envelope onion soup mix
1	bell pepper, chopped
4	cloves crushed garlic
1	quart green beans
1	quart tomatoes (fresh, if possible)
1	6-ounce can Italian tomato paste
8	ounces mushrooms
	Salt and pepper to taste
	Steamed rice

Brown beef, add onion, bell pepper, garlic, green beans, tomatoes, tomato paste, and mushrooms. Simmer 2-3 hours until meat is tender. Season with salt and pepper and serve over steamed rice. This also freezes well.

Serves 12

Bean Thread Soup

1	package bean threads
1	cup shredded raw pork
1	tablespoon soy sauce
1	tablespoon cornstarch
1	teaspoon sesame seed oil
7	cups chicken broth
1	cup bamboo shoots
1	cup mushrooms, thinly sliced
1½	teaspoons salt, or to taste
	Black pepper to taste
2	green onions, chopped

Soak bean threads in very warm water for ½ hour. When soft, cut into 2-inch sections. Shred pork or cut into matchstick slices, and mix with soy sauce, cornstarch, and sesame seed oil. Marinate at least 15 minutes. Heat chicken broth to boiling and add bean threads. Cover and cook 20 minutes or until soft. Bring to a boil again and add pork, bamboo shoots, and mushrooms. Stir with a fork to separate shreds of pork. Cook covered for 5 minutes. Add salt, pepper, and green onion. Cook uncovered for 2 minutes.

Serves 6

Bean threads are also called mung bean noodles or cellophane noodles.

Butternut Bisque

2	tablespoons butter or margarine
1	very large sweet onion, chopped
½	teaspoon chopped fresh rosemary (or dried)
2	cloves garlic, minced
5	cups peeled, diced butternut squash
1	cup peeled, diced red potatoes
5	cups chicken stock
1	teaspoon salt
	Black pepper to taste
1	cup half and half
1½	cups diced cooked ham

Melt butter in soup pot. Stir in onion and rosemary, partially cover pan, and cook over moderate heat for 10 minutes, stirring occasionally. Add garlic and cook another minute. Add squash, potatoes, chicken stock, and salt. Bring to a boil. Reduce heat and cover pot. Simmer soup for 20 minutes, or until vegetables are very soft. Remove pan from heat. Using a slotted spoon, transfer vegetables and a ladleful of broth to a food processor (do this in batches for a small processor). Purée vegetables, then stir back into broth. Add pepper, half and half, and ham. Heat several minutes before serving.

Serves 8-10

Libyan Soup

2	tablespoons extra virgin olive oil
1½	cups chopped onion
½	pound boneless lamb shoulder or dark chicken meat, finely chopped
4	medium ripe tomatoes, diced
½	3-ounce can tomato paste
2	teaspoons sweet paprika
½	teaspoon cayenne pepper or harissa to taste
½	teaspoon saffron threads
	Salt and freshly ground black pepper to taste
8	cups water
½	cup orzo, fine pearl barley, or couscous
1	cup canned chickpeas, drained
1	tablespoon finely chopped cilantro leaves
1	tablespoon finely chopped flat-leaf parsley
½	tablespoon dried mint

In a 4-quart casserole or saucepan, heat oil. Add onion and lamb or chicken, cook, stirring frequently, until just beginning to brown, about 5 minutes. Add tomatoes, tomato paste, and seasonings. Stir and add 8 cups water. Bring to a simmer and cook for 45 minutes. Add orzo and chickpeas and cook for 15 minutes until orzo is tender. Add cilantro and parsley. Taste and adjust salt, cayenne, or harissa, if desired. Add dried mint. Cook 5 minutes and serve.

Serves 6-8

This is a traditional Libyan dish.

Pot Sticker Soup

2	14-ounce cans chicken broth
2	cloves garlic, minced
1	jalapeño pepper, seeded and minced
16-18	frozen pot stickers
1½	cups fresh baby spinach (or regular spinach, stemmed and torn into pieces)
	Hot chili oil, optional

In a medium saucepan, simmer chicken broth with garlic and jalapeño over low heat for 5 minutes. Add frozen pot stickers and simmer an additional 5 minutes. Add spinach and simmer until just wilted but still bright green. Serve immediately with chili oil.

Serves 2-4

You can substitute ¼ of a 10-ounce box of frozen spinach that has been thawed, drained, and squeezed dry for fresh spinach.

Mulligatawny Soup

4	tablespoons oil
2	cups diced onion
4	large cloves garlic, minced
4	tablespoons fresh grated gingerroot
2	green serrano chili peppers, seeded and minced
½	teaspoon coarsely ground fennel seeds
⅛	teaspoon ground cloves
2	cinnamon sticks
4	bay leaves
1	teaspoon ground coriander
½	teaspoon ground cumin
¼	teaspoon ground turmeric
½	teaspoon mustard seeds (or ¼ teaspoon dry mustard)
2	cups water
2	large potatoes, cubed
3	cups chicken broth
2	cups fresh or canned diced tomatoes
1	teaspoon salt
4	boneless chicken thighs, cubed
1½	cups red lentils
2	14.5-ounce cans unsweetened coconut milk
2	tablespoons fresh lime juice
	Salt and pepper to taste
1	lime, cut into 8 wedges for garnish

Heat oil in a large soup pot. Sauté onions until translucent. Add garlic, ginger, peppers, and seasonings. Sauté for 1 minute to release flavors. Add water, chicken broth, tomatoes, and salt and simmer 5 minutes. Add potato, chicken, and lentils. Simmer 25 minutes. Carefully skim any residue on surface and discard. Remove from heat. Remove bay leaves and cinnamon sticks and discard. Remove about ½ of the solids from the soup pot and purée in a food processor to thicken (or use a stick blender in the pot). Before serving, return soup to a large saucepan and reheat over medium heat. When ready, remove from heat and stir in coconut milk and lime juice. Add salt and pepper to taste. Ladle into bowls and garnish with one lime wedge per bowl.

Serves 8

Not originally Indian cuisine, Mulligatawny was developed for the British in India and has become a standard. The name Mulligatawny means "pepper water." As with many Indian dishes, this varies substantially from region to region, with some recipes containing meat and others strictly vegetarian. There is typically a tart flavor added, sometimes using such items as apples or the combination of coconut milk and lime juice.

When using whole cloves, remove the small round piece in the middle of each clove before grinding. This will prevent a "bitter" taste.

S
O
U
P
S

West African Peanut Soup

2   onions, chopped
1   tablespoon peanut or vegetable oil
½   teaspoon cayenne pepper
1   teaspoon gingerroot, peeled and grated
1   cup chopped carrots
2   cups diced sweet potatoes
4   cups vegetable stock or water
2   cups tomato juice
1   cup smooth peanut butter
1   tablespoon sugar (optional)
1   cup chopped scallions or chives

In a large soup pot, heat oil and sauté onions until just transparent. Stir in the cayenne pepper and fresh ginger. Add the carrots and sauté two more minutes. Mix in the potatoes and stock or water, bring to a boil. Reduce heat and simmer until vegetables are tender, about 15 minutes.

In a blender or food processor, purée the vegetables with the cooking liquid and tomato juice. Return the purée to a soup pot. Stir in the peanut butter until smooth. Taste the soup. Its sweetness will depend upon the carrots and sweet potatoes. If necessary, add a little sugar to enhance the other flavors.

Reheat the soup slowly, stirring occasionally to prevent scorching. To thin soup, add more water, stock, or tomato juice. Serve topped with plenty of chopped scallions or chives.

Serves 8-10

Up to one cup white potatoes can be substituted for one cup sweet potatoes.

Remove fat from soups and stews by dropping ice cubes into the pot. Fat will cling to the cubes as it is stirred. Remove cubes before they melt. Or wrap ice cubes in cheesecloth or a paper towel and skim over the top of the pot. Fat will also cling to lettuce leaves.

Sacajawea Stew

2 tablespoons vegetable oil
¾ cup chopped onion
1 clove garlic, finely chopped
1 large red bell pepper cut into strips
2 medium poblano or Anaheim chilies, seeded and cut into strips
1 jalapeño, seeded and chopped
1 cup cubed hubbard or acorn squash (about ½ pound)
2¼ cups vegetable stock
½ teaspoon salt
½ teaspoon pepper
½ teaspoon ground coriander
1 14.5-ounce can whole kernel corn, drained
1 14.5-ounce can pinto beans, drained
1 cup yellow squash, thinly sliced
1 cup zucchini, thinly sliced

Cook onions and garlic in oil in Dutch oven over medium heat, stirring frequently, until onions are tender. Stir in bell pepper, poblano, and jalapeño chilies. Cook uncovered for 15 minutes, stirring occasionally. Stir in hubbard squash, vegetable stock, salt, pepper, and coriander. Bring to a boil. Reduce heat, cover, and simmer about 5 minutes or until squash is tender. Stir in corn, pinto beans, yellow squash, and zucchini. Cook uncovered 10 minutes, stirring occasionally, until zucchini is tender.

Serves 6

So many chilies make the stew very spicy. Choose peppers according to taste and tolerance for spiciness.

S
O
U
P
S

Corn Chowder To-Die-For

2 cups peeled, diced potatoes
6 cups chicken stock or broth
½ pound bacon, diced into ½-inch pieces
2 tablespoons butter
1 cup diced onion
½ cup flour
¾ cup diced carrot
¾ cup diced celery
2 cups canned, fresh (4 ears), or frozen corn
2 teaspoons Worcestershire sauce
Salt and white pepper to taste
1 cup heavy cream

Simmer potatoes in chicken stock until fork tender. Strain the potatoes and reserve stock. Sauté bacon until crisp, but not browned. Strain bacon fat and reserve bacon. In a sauté pan, place bacon fat, butter, and onions. Sauté until onions are transparent. Add flour to make roux, stirring until thickened. Stir in reserved chicken stock. Bring to a boil and reduce to simmer for 5 minutes. Add celery and simmer 10 minutes. Add corn, reserved bacon, and potatoes. Return to boil and test vegetables for doneness. Remove chowder from heat and add Worcestershire sauce, salt, and white pepper. Finish chowder by adding cream.

Serves 4

French Mushroom Soup

½ cup minced onion
1 stick unsalted butter, halved
6-7 tablespoons all-purpose flour
12 cups rich chicken broth
2 sprigs parsley, chopped
1 bay leaf
Pinch of thyme
3 pounds mushrooms, trimmed and sliced very thin
½ teaspoon salt
1 teaspoon lemon juice
4 egg yolks
1 cup whipping cream

Sauté onions in 4 tablespoons butter until soft. Stir in flour and cook over low heat for 4 minutes, and do not let it brown. Pour broth into a 6- or 8-quart soup pot, blend onion and flour mixture into broth, and whisk until smooth. Add half of parsley, bay leaf, and thyme. Simmer 30 minutes.

Melt remaining 4 tablespoons butter in a large pan. Toss mushrooms in butter with salt and lemon juice. Cook 5 to 7 minutes. Add mushrooms to broth and simmer 5-10 minutes or set aside if not to be used immediately.

Reheat to simmer. Beat egg yolks and cream until blended. Stir 1 cup of hot soup into the cream mixture. Add cream to the soup and heat. DO NOT simmer. Yolks will curdle if soup heats up to a simmer. Taste for seasoning. Garnish with remainder of fresh chopped parsley and serve immediately.

Serves 12

Portobello mushrooms can be substituted for regular mushrooms.

Place a raw potato in salty
soup to absorb some of the extra salt.

French Onion Soup with Caramelized Onions

CARAMELIZED ONIONS
4   large onions, sliced
1½   tablespoons olive oil

FRENCH ONION SOUP
2   14.5-ounce cans beef broth, fat skimmed
1   14.5-ounce can fat-free chicken broth
¾   cup dry sherry
1   tablespoon Worcestershire sauce
2-4 cloves garlic, minced
¾   teaspoon thyme
2   cups caramelized onions
4   ounces delicatessen sliced Swiss cheese
2   cups plain butter- or garlic-flavored croutons
4   teaspoons Parmesan cheese, or more to taste

Caramelized Onions: Peel onions and cut into ¼-inch thick slices. Place onions in a slow cooker and drizzle olive oil over the slices. Place lid on cooker and set to high, cook for 8-10 hours or until the onions caramelize to a deep brown color. Use immediately or cover and refrigerate up to 3 days. Can be frozen up to 1 month. Makes 2 cups caramelized onions with juice.

French Onion Soup: Combine beef broth, chicken broth, sherry, Worcestershire sauce, garlic, and thyme in a 4 ½- or 6-quart soup pot. Stir well, cover, and bring to a boil.

Place 4 ovenproof bowls on a large baking sheet and set aside.

When broth boils, add caramelized onions and cover. Reduce heat to low-medium and simmer for 2 minutes or until onion flavor blends with broth. Remove from heat.

Divide soup among 4 bowls. Sprinkle each bowl with ½ cup croutons. Lay a cheese slice over croutons. Sprinkle each cheese slice with 1 teaspoon Parmesan (or more to taste). Place baking sheet with prepared soup bowls under broiler until cheese melts. Serve at once. Caution: bowls will be very hot!

Serves 4

A quick and easy version of homemade French Onion Soup.

Potato and Leek Soup

¼ cup unsalted butter
3 cups chopped leeks
2 cloves garlic, minced
4 cups peeled, diced potatoes
7 cups chicken stock
1 tablespoon salt
½ teaspoon white pepper
2 cups milk
1 cup heavy cream
½ cup chopped parsley
Green onions, chopped
Paprika
Sour cream

In 5- or 6-quart stockpot, sauté leeks and garlic in butter until soft. Add potatoes, chicken stock, salt, and white pepper. Cook until potatoes are tender, 35-40 minutes. Add milk and cream. Purée half the soup, and add back to the pot. Stir in parsley.

Garnish with chopped green onions and paprika. Add a dollop of sour cream if desired.

Serves 6-8

Choose smaller leeks and use only the green bulb up to where stalks get tougher. Onions can be substituted, but will have a different flavor.

How to clean leeks: (1) Fill a long deep pan with water and add a few drops of lemon cooking juice or wine vinegar. (2) Cut off the root end and the top few inches of green. (Most recipes call for only the white part, so save the green for the broth, if you like.) Slit lengthwise, so it unscrolls. (3) Loosen the layers, and soak the leek for about 10 minutes. Rinse well with fresh water and pat dry with paper towels.

SOUPS

Chill meat or chicken broth and skim the fat
from the top before using.

Creamy Red Pepper Soup

4 tablespoons olive oil
2 onions, chopped
2 carrots, peeled and chopped
3 cloves garlic, chopped
2 teaspoons fresh thyme leaves
6 cups chicken broth
2 12-ounce jars roasted red bell peppers in water (not oil)
1 Russet potato, peeled and coarsely chopped
½ cup dry white wine
1 tablespoon sugar
  Salt and pepper
  Croutons
½ cup mascarpone cheese

Heat 2 tablespoons oil in heavy large pot over medium-high heat. Add onions, carrots, garlic, and thyme and sauté until onions are translucent (about 5 minutes).

Add broth, roasted peppers, potato, wine, and sugar. Bring to boil over high heat and then decrease to medium-low for 30 minutes, stirring occasionally. Cool and blend in blender by batches. Season to taste. Serve with dollop of cheese and croutons.

Serves 6

Bell peppers are loaded with vitamin C.

Homemade Crème Fraîche
In small bowl, combine 1 cup heavy cream with 2 tablespoons buttermilk. Stir, cover, and let stand at room temperature for 8 to 24 hours. Stir well, cover and refrigerate. Crème Fraîche can be used in cream based soups or sauces, and won't curdle when boiled.

S
O
U
P
S

Tuscan Tomato Soup

⅓ cup cold-pressed, extra virgin olive oil

3-4 cloves garlic, finely chopped

1 28-ounce can Italian plum tomatoes

Pinch of crushed chili flakes

6 cups chicken broth

1 pound very stale white or whole wheat country bread

Salt

Freshly ground pepper

6-8 large fresh basil leaves, finely shredded

Extra virgin olive oil, preferably estate Tuscan

Freshly grated Parmesan cheese

Combine oil and garlic in a heavy-bottomed soup pot. Sauté over low heat until garlic is golden, 3 to 4 minutes. Add tomatoes and chili flakes and cook over medium heat for about 10 minutes, breaking up the tomatoes with a wooden spoon. Add about 5 cups of the stock to the tomatoes. Cover and simmer for about 30 minutes.

Cut bread into 1-inch cubes. In a large bowl, add bread with just enough of the reserved stock to soften. Mash bread by pounding with the bottom of a whisk. Add to soup, stir well to combine, and gently simmer for about 10 minutes. Add a little broth or water if soup is too thick. Salt and pepper to taste.

Remove soup from heat and stir in the basil. Serve hot or allow soup to cool to room temperature. Serve with a generous drizzle of olive oil. Garnish with a few tablespoons of freshly grated Parmesan cheese.

Serves 6-8

The ingredients need to be exact, and the recipe followed closely. Substitute 1 ½ pounds of very ripe fresh tomatoes for canned tomatoes if desired. Strain through fine-holed disc of a food mill into the pot, or peel and seed tomatoes before adding.

This Tuscan soup uses all of the staples of the region: olive oil, tomatoes, and bread. It's a summer soup best served lukewarm. The recipe comes from a family in Fiesole, Italy.

SOUPS

Spicy Gazpacho with Shrimp

2   cloves garlic, minced

1   teaspoon salt

1½   cups small pieces white bread, crust removed

¼   cup red wine vinegar

⅓   cup olive oil

1   teaspoon ground cumin

2½   cups tomato juice

2   pounds tomatoes, peeled, seeded, and diced (about 3 cups)

⅔   cup finely chopped green bell pepper

⅔   cup finely chopped red bell pepper

⅓   cup minced scallions

1   cucumber, peeled, seeded, and minced

⅓   cup red onion, minced

½   pound peeled, deveined shrimp, tails removed

     Ice water

¼   cup minced fresh parsley, mint, or cilantro or a combination

     Hot pepper sauce to taste

     Salt and pepper to taste

     Croutons

     Vinegar

Combine garlic, salt, bread, vinegar, oil, cumin, and 1 cup of the tomato juice and blend until smooth. In a large bowl combine bread mixture with tomatoes, bell peppers, scallions, cucumber, and onion. Stir in remaining tomato juice. Cover and chill for 3 hours or until very cold.

Boil shrimp in water 30 seconds or until pink and just firm to the touch. Transfer to a bowl with a slotted spoon. Cool and chop shrimp. Thin soup with ice water to obtain desired consistency. Add shrimp, parsley, hot pepper sauce, salt, and pepper. Garnish with croutons. Makes about 9 cups.

Serves 6-8

Canned tomatoes may be substituted for fresh. Soup can also be made without the shrimp.

S
O
U
P
S

When using only half an onion,
save the root half. It will last longer.

Gram's Lentils

1 pound lentils, sorted for burrs
1 tablespoon baking soda
1 pound lean ground round
4 strips bacon, chopped
1 cup chopped onion
1 cup chopped green bell pepper
2 14-ounce cans diced tomatoes

Pick over the lentils, discarding any stones or bits of debris. Rinse under cold running water and drain. Mix lentils and baking soda together in large soup pot. Cover with warm water and let soak for about 1 hour. Sauté meat, bacon, onion, and bell pepper until done. Rinse lentils after soaking. Return to pan and fill with water just even with lentils. Cook separately, boiling until soft, but not mushy, about 5 to 10 minutes on low heat. Add water as needed to keep lentils moist. Combine with sautéed mixture. Add canned tomatoes. Season to taste with salt and pepper.

Serves 8-10

One of Grandmother's best old fashioned, hearty dishes. Tastes better the second or third day.

SOUPS

1 cup of dried beans or peas makes 2½ cups cooked.

Lentil and Vegetable Soup with Sweet Potatoes

2	pounds small French lentils
2-3	quarts water
3	tablespoons olive oil
12	cloves garlic, minced
2	large onions, chopped
4	carrots, peeled and chopped
6	celery stalks, chopped
2	quarts chicken stock (or vegetable stock if desired)
2	quarts vegetable stock
1-2	large sweet potatoes, peeled, ¼-inch cubes
	Basil, to taste
2	bay leaves
	Herbes de Provence, to taste
	Parsley, to taste
	Salt and freshly ground pepper

Fill a pressure cooker with 2-3 quarts of water and add lentils. Start with a cold burner, set to medium heat, and allow to pressure cook for 40 minutes. When done, set aside for 15-20 minutes before releasing the steam from the pressure cooker. The lentils will soften a lot. Drain.

In a separate skillet, heat olive oil on low and sauté garlic until soft. Increase heat to medium, add chopped onions, and cook until translucent. Remove garlic and onions, set aside. To the skillet, add a little more olive, oil and sauté carrots and celery.

In a large stockpot, combine onions, garlic, lentils, carrots, and celery. Add chicken stock and vegetable stock, basil, bay leaves, herbes de Provence, and parsley. Bring to a boil. Add sweet potatoes and cook on medium until the potatoes are cooked through. Add more water or stock to thin to desired consistency. Salt and pepper to taste.

Serves 8-10

For an alternative to vegetable stock, reserve 2 quarts of water from steaming vegetables or boiling potatoes.

The pressure cooker gives the lentils a head start, and it's a real timesaver for cooking in the mountains.

78

S
O
U
P
S

Caribbean Chili

¼	cup vegetable oil
4	medium onions, chopped
¼	cup crushed garlic
1-2	tablespoons diced and seeded habanero pepper
¼	cup chili powder
¼	cup ground cumin
2	tablespoons sugar
2	teaspoons salt
2	teaspoons pepper
1½	cups orange juice
¾	cup lime juice
3	teaspoons orange zest
3	teaspoons lime zest
1	28-ounce can crushed tomatoes
5-6	14.5-ounce cans black beans, drained
6	cups water
	Sour cream
	Scallions
	Lime

In a large soup pot, sauté onions in oil until browned, 8 to 10 minutes. Add garlic and habanero pepper and cook for 1 minute. Add remaining ingredients; stir, and simmer on low heat for 1 to 2 hours. Serve with sour cream, chopped scallions, and lime.

Serves 10-12

This is a spicy black bean soup more like a chili. It has a wonderful citrus flavor.

Mexican Pork Green Chili

2	pounds pork shoulder or tenderloin, cubed to desired size
4	tablespoons minced garlic
	Salt and pepper
4	medium tomatoes, diced
1	medium onion, diced
1	pound frozen hot green chilies
1	pound frozen mild green chilies
1	cup flour
1	32-ounce can tomato juice
3	cups water

Brown pork with garlic, salt, and pepper in a small amount of cooking oil. Add water just to cover and simmer for 1 hour until meat is almost tender. Add tomatoes, onion and green chilies. Cover and simmer for 1 more hour. In small iron skillet, brown flour in as much oil as needed to make a roux, stirring constantly. Add tomato juice and flour roux to pork mixture. Add salt, pepper, and garlic to taste.

Serves 6-8

Use fresh roasted green chilies when available. Add diced potatoes and/or pinto beans to add more body and cut the hot flavor, if too spicy.

SOUPS

Cha-Ching Chili

3   pounds hand-cut cubed tenderloin or lean, coarse ground beef
    Cooking spray
2   medium-sweet or white onions, chopped
1   3-4-ounce canned, fresh, or frozen diced green chilies
1   tablespoon bacon fat or cooking oil
1   14.5-ounce can beef broth
1   14.5-ounce can chicken broth
1¼   cups water
1   8-ounce can tomato sauce
6   tomatillos or Roma tomatoes, peeled and chopped
2   tablespoons arrowroot powder or masa harina (or ¾ cup cooked and mashed pintos or Anasazi beans)
1   teaspoon Hungarian paprika
2   tablespoons pure New Mexican chili powder (medium hot)
2   tablespoons ground cumin
3   tablespoons blended chili powder
¼   teaspoon white pepper
½   teaspoon brown sugar
¼   teaspoon pequin or cayenne chili powder (optional)
5   cloves garlic, minced
    Salt to taste

OPTIONAL ADD-INS AND GARNISH
1   14.5-ounce can diced tomatoes
1   14.5-ounce can pinto or kidney beans, drained
    Grated Monterey Jack or Cheddar cheese

Brown meat, half at a time, in frying pan or Dutch oven coated with cooking spray. Drain and set aside. Brown onions and green chilies using bacon fat (or oil) for 3-5 minutes over medium heat. Combine meat, onions, and green chilies in 5-quart Dutch oven or heavy stockpot. In a bowl, blend all spices. Add 2 tablespoons of spice mixture to meat. Over medium heat, "burn" spices into meat-onion mixture (about 3 minutes). Add broth and water and simmer for 1 hour. Add tomato sauce, tomatoes, and balance of spices. Cook until meat is tender (30 minutes for ground meat, 1 hour for cubed meat). Add more chili spice and salt to taste. Add pequin/cayenne or hot sauce to increase heat level if desired. In a small cup, blend arrowroot or masa harina powder with 2 tablespoons of water and slowly pour into pot while stirring, or mash some of the cooked beans and stir in to thicken the mixture.

For more "home style" chili, add 1 can diced tomatoes and 1 can pinto or kidney beans, or cook a package of Anasazi beans separately and add appropriate amount about ½ hour before serving. Serve with cornbread or crackers. Garnish with grated Cheddar or Monterey Jack cheese.

Serves 10-12

Replace ground spices every 6 months or so
as they often lose flavor over time.

Chili Blanco

2	quarts water
3	whole skinless chicken breasts
¼	cup vegetable oil
1	medium onion, chopped
1	medium green bell pepper, diced
3	cloves garlic, minced
2	tablespoons diced and seeded jalapeño pepper
2	32-ounce boxes chicken broth
2	teaspoons lime juice
2	teaspoons coarse salt
3	tablespoons cornstarch
2	tablespoons ground cumin
2½	tablespoons ground chili powder
2	teaspoons ground paprika
2	teaspoons dried basil
1½	teaspoons ground red pepper
4	tomatillos, husks removed, diced
1	4-ounce can diced green chilies, drained
2	15-ounce cans navy beans or small white beans, drained
1	15-ounce can dark red kidney beans, drained
2	teaspoons freshly minced cilantro
	Shredded Cheddar or jack cheese and sour cream, for garnish, optional
	Tortilla chips

Bring 2 quarts salted water to boil, place chicken breasts in pot and boil over medium heat until just tender, about 45 minutes. Remove chicken and set aside to cool. In 5-quart or larger stockpot, heat oil over medium heat. Add onions and sauté along with bell pepper, garlic, and jalapeño, until vegetables are tender. Add chicken broth, lime juice, salt, cornstarch, and seasonings, except cilantro. Add tomatillos and diced green chilies to pot. Bring to boil, lower heat, and simmer for ½ hour. Add beans and cooked chicken to chili, bring to boil, and simmer 10 minutes. Add minced cilantro. Serve topped with cheese and sour cream if desired, with tortilla chips on the side.

Serves 10-12

Substitute ½ cup fresh or frozen diced green chilies if available.

SOUPS

Store freshly cut basil in a glass with water covering only stems. Keep on the kitchen counter, change water occasionally. It will keep for weeks. Never put freshly cut basil in the refrigerator.

Ed's Green Chili

10   pounds pork, cut into bite-size pieces
4   27-ounce cans whole green chilies, with juice
1½   tablespoons chili flakes
1½   tablespoons caribe (crushed New Mexico red chilies)
½   teaspoon cayenne pepper
1   teaspoon garlic pepper
1   teaspoon chili powder
1   teaspoon garlic salt
1   teaspoon seasoned salt
¾   tablespoon bacon grease
      Jalapeño pepper, sliced (optional)
4   bunches green onions, chopped
2   14.5-ounce cans chopped tomatoes, drained
1   7-ounce can diced green chilies
1   cup flour
3   chicken bouillon cubes
      Pinch of thyme, cumin, and oregano
      Cold water

Pour juice from peppers into 16-quart pot with bacon grease, chili flakes, caribe, cayenne pepper, garlic pepper, chili powder, garlic salt, and seasoned salt and bring to a boil. Stirring, add meat and cover. Lift lid only occasionally to stir until meat is done. Add fresh jalapeño slices. Dice green chilies and add enough water to fill pot ¾ full. Bring to a boil and add onions, tomatoes, and canned chopped chilies. Mix ¾ to 1 cup flour and cold water for thickening. Pour the roux into simmering chili mixture. Stirring over low heat, add chicken bouillon and a pinch of thyme, cumin, and oregano. Let simmer for a few hours.

Serves 20-24

For milder chili, omit jalapeño slices.

South Park Chicken Soup

2   tablespoons vegetable oil
1   pound skinless, boneless chicken breasts, cut into ½-inch pieces
¼   cup onion, finely diced
¼   teaspoon garlic powder
½   teaspoon salt
½   teaspoon chili powder
⅛   teaspoon red pepper
1   14.5-ounce can chicken broth
1   15.25-ounce can corn kernels, with juice
1   14.5-ounce can black beans, rinsed and drained
1   14.5-ounce Mexican style stewed tomatoes
      Tortilla chips

Heat oil in stockpot over medium heat, add chicken, and cook for 3-4 minutes until opaque. Add onion, garlic powder, salt, chili powder, and red pepper and cook for 1-2 minutes, stirring frequently. Add broth, corn, beans, and tomatoes. Increase heat to high and bring to boil. Reduce heat, cover, and simmer until chicken is tender, about 15 minutes. Serve with tortilla chips.

Serves 6-8

Two cups water with 2 teaspoons chicken bouillon can be substituted for canned chicken broth.

Corny Tortilla Soup

2	cups cooked or grilled diced chicken
1	14.5-ounce can chicken broth
3	cups water
1	cup peeled, diced canned or fresh tomatoes
1	medium onion, chopped
1	celery stalk, thinly sliced
1	4-ounce can chopped green chilies
1	carrot, peeled and sliced
2	cloves garlic, crushed
1½	cups tomato juice
2	teaspoons Worcestershire sauce
1	teaspoon ground cumin
1	teaspoon chili powder
1	teaspoon salt
½	teaspoon crushed red pepper
1	jalapeño pepper, seeded and diced
1	10-ounce can corn, drained
2	tablespoons fresh cilantro, chopped
3	corn tortillas cut into ½-inch strips
¼	cup shredded Asadero or Monterey Jack cheese
1	ripe avocado, peeled and diced

Sauté seasoned chicken breasts or tenders in a large skillet in a small amount of oil until browned and set aside (or use cooked chicken already prepared). In a stockpot, put chicken broth, water, tomatoes, onions, celery, chilies, carrots, garlic, tomato juice, Worcestershire sauce, and spices. Bring to boil. Reduce heat and simmer, partially covered, for 30 minutes. Add chicken, jalapeño, corn, and cilantro and simmer 10 more minutes. Lightly toast tortilla strips on cookie sheet in oven or lightly fry in skillet in a small amount of oil until crispy. Place a small handful of strips in the bottom of a large soup bowl, add about 2 tablespoons grated cheese, and ladle hot soup on top. Garnish with toasted tortilla strips, chopped cilantro, and avocado chunks.

Serves 6-8

Adjust the "heat" several ways: use canned tomatoes, eliminate the jalapeño (or just use for garnish), or adjust the amount of red pepper.

SOUPS

Substitute for Chili Powder
3 tablespoons paprika
1 tablespoon ground cumin
2 tablespoons oregano
1 teaspoon red or cayenne pepper
1-2 teaspoons garlic

Baked Potato Soup

4-6 russet potatoes, peeled and cut into 1½-inch cubes
6 strips bacon
½ stick butter
½ onion, finely chopped
2 tablespoons flour
3 cups whole milk
1½ cups heavy cream
　 Salt
　 White pepper
　 Hot pepper sauce

GARNISH
　 Grated medium Cheddar cheese
½ cup green onions, finely chopped
　 Sour cream

In stock pot, boil potatoes in salted water until tender, but not mushy. Drain and set aside. Cook bacon until crisp, crumble, and set aside.

Melt butter in large pot over medium-low heat. Add onion and sauté until barely wilted, 3-5 minutes. Slowly stir in flour and cook until thickened, 2-3 minutes. Slowly add milk and cream until medium sauce consistency. Add potatoes and simmer over low heat until heated through. Season with salt and pepper to taste. Add a few dashes of hot pepper sauce.

Purée the entire soup in the blender or food processor, return to pot, and finish heating. For a chunkier soup, purée only half of the mixture.

Pour soup into warm bowls and garnish with cheese, bacon, sour cream and green onions. Serve immediately.

Serves 4-6

84

S
O
U
P
S

Boiling point is much lower at altitude than at sea level. It's lowered 1°F for approximately every 500 feet of ascent.

PASTA

Contents

Angel Hair Pasta with Sun-Dried Tomatoes and Goat Cheese

1	10-ounce jar sun-dried tomatoes packed in oil, chopped, reserve oil
1	small onion, chopped
4	cloves garlic, minced
¼	cup tomato paste
⅔	cup dry white wine
8	ounces angel hair pasta
2	ounces goat cheese, coarsely crumbled
2	tablespoons fresh Italian parsley, chopped
	Salt and freshly ground pepper to taste

In a large skillet over medium heat, warm 2 tablespoons of oil from the jar of sun-dried tomatoes. Add onion and sauté until tender, about 3 minutes. Stir in garlic and sauté until fragrant, about 1 minute. Add tomato paste, cook for 2 minutes, stirring constantly. Add wine and sun-dried tomatoes, simmer until liquid reduces by half, about 2 minutes.

In a large pot bring salted water to a full boil. Add pasta and cook until al dente, stirring occasionally, about 10 minutes. Drain, reserving ½ cup cooking liquid. Add pasta to tomato mixture and toss to coat, adding some reserved liquid to moisten. Season with salt and pepper. Sprinkle with goat cheese and parsley, and stir. Serve in bowls.

Serves 4

Linguine With White Clam Sauce

4	cloves garlic, crushed
¼	cup extra virgin olive oil
¼	cup canola oil
1-2	tablespoons flour
4	6.5-ounce cans chopped clams with liquid
1½	cups chopped fresh parsley
½	teaspoon salt
¼	teaspoon fresh ground pepper
16	ounces cooked linguine, drained

In a medium skillet, sauté garlic in oil on low heat until barely golden. Blend in flour and cook for 2 minutes, stirring constantly. Gradually stir in clams with liquid; add parsley, salt and pepper. Cook over medium low heat, stirring constantly, until sauce is thickened. Serve over linguine, cooked al dente.

Serves 6-8

It's a quick, easy, elegant dish to serve for guests. The clam sauce can be doubled and frozen for up to 4 weeks.

Shrimp Nashville

Tequila Marinated Shrimp in a Spicy Cream Sauce

1½ pounds shrimp, peeled and deveined

2 ounces tequila

2 limes

1 tablespoon cilantro

2 tablespoons olive oil

Zest of 1 orange

1 tablespoon honey or brown sugar

1 dried habanero pepper, crushed (or one jalapeño, seeded and chopped)

½ stick butter

2 tablespoons flour

1½ cups milk or cream

¼ cup Romano cheese, grated

1 cup pepper jack cheese, grated

4 ounces angel hair pasta, cooked

In a bowl add tequila, lime juice, chopped cilantro, olive oil, orange zest, honey, and crushed pepper. Add the shrimp and marinate. In a saucepan melt butter over medium low heat, add flour, and stir for 2-3 minutes until slightly browned. Slowly add milk or cream, cooking until thickened. Gradually add cheeses and stir until completely melted. Reduce heat to simmer. Add shrimp and marinade to cream sauce. Stir constantly. Cook until shrimp are just opaque, do not overcook. Garnish with crushed habanero pepper or chopped jalapeño pepper. Serve over angel hair pasta.

Serves 4

This dish was invented one night in Nashville out of items that happened to be in the refrigerator, and so, "Shrimp Nashville" was born.

Bun Bun Noodles

⅓ cup peanut butter

3 tablespoons sugar

¼ cup soy sauce

1 teaspoon red pepper flakes

1 tablespoon minced garlic

3 tablespoons corn oil

3 tablespoons sesame oil

10 ounces angel hair pasta, cooked

1 carrot, finely grated

Sesame seeds

Chopped green onions to garnish

Chopped peanuts to garnish

In a saucepan heat peanut butter over medium low heat until soft, reduce heat to low, stir in sugar, soy sauce, red pepper flakes, garlic, and corn oil. Remove from heat, add sesame oil and cooked pasta. Gently mix to thoroughly coat pasta. Garnish with finely grated carrot, sesame seeds, chopped green onion, and chopped peanuts to taste. Let stand at room temperature until ready to serve.

Serves 4-6

Linguini with Puttanesca Sauce and Grilled Tuna

1	small tuna steak
1	tablespoon olive oil
¼	cup chopped onion
1	clove garlic, crushed
1	12-ounce can crushed tomatoes or Italian stewed tomatoes
¼	cup black olives, sliced
1	tablespoon red wine
1	medium bay leaf
¾	teaspoon chopped fresh oregano (¼ teaspoon dry oregano)
¼	teaspoon red pepper flakes
1	pound linguini or fettuccini
2	tablespoons or more fresh parsley, chopped
	Fresh Parmesan cheese, grated

Preheat grill to medium heat or preheat broiler. Grill or broil fresh tuna steak, about 10 minutes per inch of thickness, turning once. Cool and gently pull apart into flakes. To make sauce, heat oil in a medium-sized skillet, add onion, and cook until softened. Add garlic, crushed tomatoes, black olives, red wine, bay leaf, oregano, and red pepper flakes. Bring to a boil, reduce heat, and simmer about 20 minutes, add tuna. Prepare pasta according to directions. Toss pasta with sauce. Garnish with fresh parsley and Parmesan cheese.

Serves 6

A healthy alternative. Don't let the tuna scare you.

To shorten cooking time use 12 ounces water-packed albacore canned tuna, drained, and leave chunky.

Pasta Fresco

1 ¾	cups all purpose flour, plus extra for dusting
2	eggs, lightly beaten
	Salt

Sift the flour and salt and mound on a large cutting board. Make a well in the center of the flour and add the eggs. Using a fork, gradually incorporate the flour and eggs together. Knead the dough for 10 minutes. If the dough is too soft, add flour; if too firm, add water. Shape the dough into a ball and rest for 15 minutes. Roll the dough on a lightly floured surface or use a pasta machine to make a thin sheet. Cut into desired shapes.

Serves 6

Creole Pasta

½ cup boneless, skinless, julienned chicken breasts
2½ teaspoons Creole seasoning
1 tablespoon olive oil
2 ounces chopped andouille sausage
½ pound peeled and deveined medium shrimp
¼ cup chopped green onions
1 tablespoon minced garlic
1½ cups heavy cream
½ teaspoon salt
¼ teaspoon hot sauce
¼ teaspoon Worcestershire sauce
½ pound fettuccine
½ cup Parmesan cheese, freshly grated

Toss chicken strips with 1 teaspoon Creole seasoning. In a large skillet over high heat, heat 1 tablespoon oil. Add seasoned chicken and sauté, stirring occasionally, for about 1 minute. Add andouille, cook and stir for 1 minute. Add shrimp and remaining 1½ teaspoons Creole seasoning, sauté for 1 minute. Stir in green onions, garlic, and cream, cook for 2 minutes. Stir in the Worcestershire sauce, hot sauce, salt, and ¼ cup Parmesan and simmer for 3 minutes.

Cook pasta in a large pot of boiling salted water. Drain and add to sauce. Toss until pasta is heated through and thoroughly blended with sauce, about 1 minute. Remove from heat. Makes about 5 cups. To serve, allow 1¼ cups per portion in pasta bowls. Sprinkle each portion with remaining Parmesan.

Serves 4

90

Spicy Vegetable Couscous

2 tablespoons olive oil
½ cup diced yellow summer squash
½ cup diced zucchini
½ cup diced red onion
1 clove garlic, minced
1 cup chickpeas (garbanzos)
½ teaspoon ground cumin
½ teaspoon curry powder
½ teaspoon dried red pepper flakes
½ teaspoon salt
Freshly ground black pepper, to taste
2 cups couscous, cooked in chicken stock
¼ cup chopped fresh parsley

Preheat oven to 350°F. In a large skillet heat the oil, squash, zucchini, red onions, and garlic. Sauté 5 minutes. Stir in chickpeas and spices. Gently stir in cooked couscous. Cook until hot, about 8 minutes. Spoon into a large casserole dish, dot with butter, and bake in preheated oven for 15 minutes or until hot. Garnish with parsley.

Serves 4

Couscous is quick cooking. Try making this with quinoa, another grain, sold in the health food section of the supermarket.

Castle Cannelloni with White Cream Sauce

MEAT FILLING

4	cloves garlic
1	medium onion
2	tablespoons butter
2	tablespoons olive oil
1	pound ground meat or ground elk
1	package chopped spinach, thawed
½	teaspoon oregano
	Salt and pepper to taste
2	eggs, beaten
2	tablespoons cream
6	tablespoons freshly grated Parmesan cheese
1	package cannelloni for stuffing, cooked and drained

CREAM SAUCE

8	tablespoons butter
8	tablespoons flour
2	cups milk
2	cups heavy cream
1-1½	teaspoons salt to taste
	White pepper to taste
	Dash of cayenne

TOMATO SAUCE

2	tablespoons olive oil
1	small onion
2	1-pound cans tomatoes
3	tablespoons tomato paste
1	teaspoon basil
1	teaspoon sugar
½	teaspoon salt
	Black pepper to taste
3-4	tablespoons freshly grated Parmesan cheese
	Butter

Preheat oven to 350°F.

Meat Filling: Purée garlic and onions in blender. Melt butter and olive oil in a heavy skillet. Add onion-garlic mixture and ground meat; cook until meat is well done. Add spinach and cook until most of the moisture is gone. Add oregano, salt and pepper to taste. Cool. Mix together eggs and cream. Add egg mixture and cheese to spinach mixture. Stuff pasta tubes with filling.

Cream sauce: In a medium saucepan, melt butter and add flour. Cook 2 minutes; add milk and cream, stirring constantly until thick. Add salt, pepper, and cayenne to taste.

Tomato sauce: In a medium skillet over low heat, heat olive oil. In a blender, purée onions and 1 can of tomatoes. Add to heated olive oil. Blend remaining tomatoes and tomato paste. Add this mixture to skillet with basil, sugar, salt; and pepper, simmer, partially covered, for 30 minutes.

To assemble the casserole, glaze the bottom of a 9x13-inch ovenproof glass dish with the tomato sauce. Put in one layer of stuffed cannelloni, cover with cream sauce and top with tomato sauce. Sprinkle with 3-4 tablespoons Parmesan cheese and dot with butter. Cook in oven until bubbly and brown.

Serves 6-8

Manicotti

CRÊPES
1 cup water
3 eggs
1 cup flour

FILLING
1 pound ricotta cheese
1 tablespoon chopped fresh parsley
¼ cup Parmesan cheese
Salt and pepper to taste
⅓ cup mozzarella cheese, shredded
Marinara or tomato meat sauce

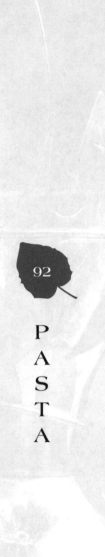

92

P
A
S
T
A

In a small bowl, mix water and flour; add eggs and beat until smooth. Lightly grease a 6 inch non-stick skillet. Heat skillet and pour a scant ¼ cup of batter into pan. Quickly lift pan from burner and tip in several directions to cover the bottom of pan. Return to burner. Cook over medium heat until batter is set and starts to dry around the edges. There should be no wet batter on top. Flip crêpe over onto lightly greased waxed paper or foil. This recipe should make 12-13 crêpes.

In a medium-sized bowl, combine all filling ingredients; mix well. Spread about 2 tablespoons of filling on a crêpe; fold each side over to the middle, overlapping edges a bit.

Preheat oven to 350°F. Using your favorite marinara or tomato meat sauce, cover bottom of a 9x12 inch baking dish with sauce. Place manicotti in single layer, seam side down (not too tightly packed), in dish; cover with sauce and Parmesan cheese. Bake in oven until bubbly, approximately 30 minutes. Delicious served with green salad and Italian bread for an entrée, or smaller portions may be served before a poultry or roast beef entrée. Can be frozen before baking; defrost completely and bake as directed.

Serves 4-6

Noodles, spaghetti and other starches will not boil over if the inside of the pot is rubbed with vegetable oil.

Pasta alla Fiorentina

SAUCE

1	pound ground sausage meat
2	pounds ground beef
1	cup chopped onion
½	teaspoon dried rosemary
½	teaspoon red pepper flakes
2	cloves garlic, minced
1	28-ounce can crushed tomatoes, very well drained
1	cup red wine
½	cup water
1½	teaspoons dried basil
1½	teaspoons dried marjoram
½	teaspoon ground oregano
½	teaspoon savory

PASTA

16	ounces farfalle (bow tie pasta), cooked and well drained
3	packages frozen chopped spinach, defrosted
2½	cups sour cream
½	pound provolone cheese, sliced
1½	cups grated Parmesan cheese

Preheat oven to 375°F. To make the sauce, use a large stock pot to brown sausage, ground beef, and onion. Drain fat. Add rosemary, red pepper, and garlic. Stir in tomatoes, wine, water, and spices, simmer, stirring occasionally, for about 45 minutes. To assemble, mix sauce with cooked, drained pasta. Place ¼ of the pasta mixture in each of two (2) 9x13-inch baking dishes. Layer with spinach. Dot with sour cream and smooth out. Place a layer of provolone cheese slices on top of sour cream. Sprinkle with half the Parmesan cheese. Repeat the layers, except for the provolone-it only goes on the first layer! At this point, pasta can be baked or placed in the refrigerator. Bake uncovered for 40-50 minutes. If taken from refrigerator to oven, allow an additional 15-20 minutes of cooking time.

Serves 18-24

Creamy Lemon Pasta

3	tablespoons unsalted butter
¾	cup heavy cream
	Juice and zest from 1 lemon
¾	teaspoon salt
	Pepper to taste
	Pasta
	Ingredients of choice

Heat butter and cream over moderately low heat until butter is melted. Stir in lemon juice, zest, salt, and pepper. Heat 1-2 more minutes then remove from heat. Stir in hot cooked pasta and additional ingredients.

Serves 4

This recipe is great for the summer and when you wish it were summer!

Suggestions: linguine with chicken and red and yellow peppers, or bowties with 2-inch pieces of fresh asparagus.

Best Ever Baked Ziti

1   pound ziti pasta, uncooked
1½   tablespoons olive oil
1   onion, sliced
1   teaspoon minced fresh
      rosemary
4   cloves garlic, chopped
½   pound ground beef
½   pound ground pork sausage
1   26-ounce jar spaghetti sauce
      Salt to taste
6   ounces provolone cheese, sliced
¾   cup sour cream
¾   cup cottage cheese
6   ounces mozzarella cheese,
      shredded
2   tablespoons grated Parmesan
      cheese

Preheat oven to 350°F. Bring a large pot of lightly salted water to a boil. Cook pasta in boiling water until al dente and drain. In a very large skillet heat oil over medium heat. Cook onions in oil until tender. Stir in rosemary and garlic. Transfer to a small bowl. Place ground beef and sausage in skillet, cook over medium heat until evenly browned. Stir in onion mixture and spaghetti sauce. Season to taste with salt. Reduce heat to low and simmer for 10 minutes. Grease a 9x13-inch baking dish. Layer ½ of the cooked pasta, provolone cheese, sour cream, cottage cheese, and a little less than ½ of the meat mixture. Then layer the rest of the pasta, mozzarella cheese, remaining meat mixture, and Parmesan cheese. Bake in preheated oven for 20-30 minutes, or until heated through and cheeses are melted.

Serves 12

This has flavor and yields a great amount. Try this recipe, it is great for big groups.

P
A
S
T
A

When cooking pasta, 8 ounces of uncooked pasta makes 4 cups cooked pasta.

Incredible Stuffed Shells

1	medium round eggplant
3	large red bell peppers
1	head garlic
½	pound Italian sausage, mild or hot
2	teaspoons salt
2	teaspoons pepper
½	pound ricotta cheese
1	28-ounce can diced tomatoes in their juice, puréed
2	tablespoons olive oil
1	teaspoon fresh basil, chopped
1	clove garlic, crushed
1	teaspoon salt
1	teaspoon black pepper
½	cup white wine
12	ounces giant pasta shells
	Salt and fresh ground pepper
½	cup fresh Parmesan cheese, grated

Preheat oven 400°F. To prepare roasted vegetables, make a few small slices in eggplant and peppers and place on greased baking sheet in preheated oven. Slice top off of the garlic head. Drizzle with olive oil, wrap in aluminum foil and place on baking sheet with other vegetables. Roast for 40-50 minutes or until the skin on the vegetables is slightly blackened and garlic is soft. Remove the vegetables from the oven. Reduce heat to 350°F. Peel the skins off of the grilled vegetables and garlic and set aside. In a frying pan, cook the Italian sausage draining fat, let cool. In a food processor, combine cooked Italian sausage, eggplant, peppers, garlic, and salt and pepper to taste. Process to a coarse chop. Fold in ricotta cheese and refrigerate. In a large pot, heat water to boiling. Add a teaspoon of salt and 12 ounces of giant pasta shells. Cook al dente. Drain and rinse in cold water. Set aside. Prepare the sauce. In a skillet, sauté 1 clove of crushed garlic in oil. Add the puréed tomatoes, basil, and wine. Simmer for 35 minutes. To assemble, stuff shells with ricotta filling. Using a flat pan or dish, pour some sauce on bottom of pan. Place shells over sauce in a single layer and cover with the remaining sauce. Sprinkle with ½ cup of Parmesan cheese and bake at 350°F for 20-30 minutes until hot and bubbly. This dish is best made a day before company is expected. Makes about 32 stuffed shells.

Serves 6-8

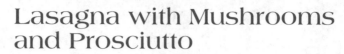

Lasagna with Mushrooms and Prosciutto

MUSHROOM FILLING

1½	ounces imported dried porcini mushrooms
1½	pounds fresh mushrooms, sliced
2	cups warm water (120°F)
¼	cup vegetable oil
6	tablespoons butter
⅓	cup onion, finely chopped
⅓	cup canned Italian plum tomatoes, drained and chopped
2	tablespoons chopped Italian parsley
	Salt and pepper

BÉCHAMEL SAUCE

4	tablespoons butter
3	tablespoons flour
2	cups milk
¼	teaspoon salt

REMAINING INGREDIENTS

1	package fresh lasagna noodles
¾	pound Prosciutto, thinly sliced
1	cup Parmesan cheese, freshly grated plus extra for the table
4	tablespoons butter

96

P
A
S
T
A

Preheat oven to 400°F. Soak the dried mushrooms for 30 minutes in a small bowl with 2 cups of warm water. Gently lift the mushrooms from the water, reserving the water. Rinse the mushrooms several times to remove any remaining grit. Chop into large pieces, set aside. Filter the water in a strainer lined with paper towel. Reserve for later use.

In a large sauté pan, heat the oil and butter. Add onions and cook over medium heat until onions are translucent. Add the porcini mushrooms, filtered water, tomatoes, and parsley. Stir well and cover the pan with the cover slightly ajar. Turn the heat to medium low.

When the liquid is evaporated, add the sliced fresh mushrooms and turn the heat to high. Cook uncovered, stirring frequently, for 7-8 minutes until all the liquid evaporates. Remove from heat and season with salt and freshly ground pepper to taste.

In a sauce pan over medium heat prepare the béchamel sauce. Melt 4 tablespoons of butter. Add 3 tablespoons of flour and blend together with a whisk. Add ¼ teaspoon of salt. Gradually add the milk, pouring slowly and whisking continuously. Continue cooking until the sauce thickens. Keep warm over low heat, stirring occasionally.

To prepare the lasagna, thickly coat the bottom of a 9x13-inch lasagna pan with butter. Line the bottom of the pan with a layer of pasta. Overlap the pasta no more than ¼ inch. Spread a thin layer of mushrooms over the pasta. Spread a thin layer of béchamel sauce over the mushroom mixture. Add a layer of sliced Prosciutto and sprinkle with cheese. Continue building layers and repeating the sequence until you reach 6 layers of pasta. On the top layer spread béchamel, sprinkle with cheese, and dot with 2 tablespoons of butter. Bake in preheated oven for 15 minutes until a light golden crust forms on the top. If there is no crust after 15 minutes, increase the temperature another 50°F for the next 5 minutes. Remove lasagna and let rest for 10 minutes before serving. Serve directly from the pan with grated Parmesan cheese on the side.

Serves 8

Eggplant Parmesan Lasagna

2   large egg whites
1   large egg
1   1-pound eggplant, cut crosswise into ¼-inch thick slices
1   cup Italian seasoned breadcrumbs
3   tablespoons all-purpose flour
12 cooked lasagna noodles
1   12-ounce carton 1% low-fat cottage cheese
2   cups shredded part-skim mozzarella, divided
1   teaspoon dried oregano, or 1 tablespoon fresh chopped oregano
1   teaspoon dried basil, or 1 tablespoon fresh chopped basil
15 ounces part-skim ricotta cheese
1   large egg white
1   26-ounce jar tomato-basil pasta sauce
5   tablespoons fresh Parmesan cheese, grated and divided
    Cooking spray

97

P
A
S
T
A

Preheat oven to 450°F. In a small bowl, whisk to combine 2 egg whites and egg. Dredge 1 eggplant slice in flour, dip in egg mixture, and then in breadcrumbs. Place slices in a single layer on a baking sheet coated with cooking spray. Repeat procedure with remaining eggplant, flour, egg mixture, and breadcrumbs. Coat tops of slices with cooking spray. Bake in preheated oven for 20 minutes, turning eggplant after 10 minutes. Remove from baking sheet. Cool. Reduce oven temperature to 375°F.

Combine cottage cheese, 1 cup shredded mozzarella, oregano, basil, ricotta, 3 tablespoons Parmesan, and 1 egg white in a large bowl. Spread ¼ cup pasta sauce in the bottom of a 9x13-inch baking dish coated with cooking spray. Arrange 4 lasagna noodles slightly overlapping over the pasta sauce. Top with half of the cheese mixture, half of eggplant slices, and ¾ cup pasta sauce. Repeat layers, ending with noodles. Spread remaining pasta sauce over noodles. Sprinkle with 1 cup mozzarella and 2 tablespoons Parmesan. Cover and bake at 375°F for 15 minutes. Uncover and bake an additional 35 minutes or until cheese melts. Let stand 5 minutes before serving.

Serves 9

Ultimate Spaghetti Sauce

1½   pounds bulk sausage
2½   pounds ground beef
2   large onions, chopped
2   ribs celery, chopped
1   green bell pepper, chopped
3   cloves garlic, minced
2   6-ounce cans tomato paste
    Dry red wine
1   28-ounce can crushed
      tomatoes
2   15-ounce cans tomato sauce
    1 pound mushrooms, sliced
    Zest of one lemon
    Pinch of sugar (optional)
2   tablespoons chopped fresh
      parsley
2   tablespoons chopped fresh
      basil
2   tablespoons fresh oregano
    Salt and pepper
4   tablespoons Worcestershire
      sauce
2   tablespoons soy sauce
12   ounces vermicelli, cooked al
      dente
    Romano cheese, freshly grated
    Parmesan cheese, freshly
      grated

In a large pot, slowly cook sausage and ground beef until brown. Add onions, celery, bell pepper, and garlic. Simmer until onions are translucent. Add tomato paste, cook until it turns dark red (a few minutes). Using small tomato paste can, measure and add 2 cans of red wine. Add crushed tomatoes and tomato sauce. Cook about 15 minutes. Add mushrooms, lemon zest, sugar, herbs, salt and pepper, Worcestershire sauce, and soy sauce. Uncover and slowly simmer for as long as you have time; the longer the better. Stir occasionally. Add grated cheese and serve over vermicelli. Sprinkle additional cheese over each serving.

Serves 6

This recipe typifies the traditional sauce. It has lots of ingredients and is a simmer-all-day sauce.

P
A
S
T
A

Never heat pesto sauce, the
basil will turn black and taste bitter.

Best Lasagna Cheese Sauce Ever

¼ cup butter
¼ cup flour
½ teaspoon salt
¼ teaspoon pepper
⅛ teaspoon nutmeg
2 cups milk
1½ cups grated mozzarella cheese
¼ cup grated Parmesan cheese

In a saucepan melt butter over low heat. Stir in flour, salt, pepper, and nutmeg. Cook for 2-3 minutes, stirring constantly. Stir in milk slowly. Cook over medium heat for 3-4 minutes, stirring constantly. Stir in mozzarella and Parmesan. Cook over low heat, stirring constantly, until completely melted. One recipe of this sauce will suffice for one small to medium lasagna. Double if necessary.

Serves 6

Lasagna: Preheat oven to 350°F. Layer sauce with lasagna noodles, meat, or blanched vegetables of choice (spinach, zucchini, etc.), and red sauce of your choosing. Top lasagna with 1 cup mozzarella and ¼ cup Parmesan. Bake 40-50 minutes until cheese is golden.

P
A
S
T
A

Lentil Spaghetti Sauce

2 tablespoons olive oil
1 onion, chopped
4 cloves garlic, minced
½ pound fresh mushrooms, sliced
1 16-ounce can tomato sauce
6 ounces tomato paste
1 cup water
½ cup lentils, washed
1½ teaspoons dry basil
1 teaspoon dried oregano
1 tablespoon sugar
1 bay leaf
½ teaspoon salt
⅛ teaspoon black pepper
12 ounces vermicelli, cooked al dente

In a skillet, sauté the onion, garlic, and mushrooms in olive oil until just tender. Add the tomato sauce, tomato paste, water, lentils, basil, oregano, sugar, bay leaf, salt and pepper and simmer for 30-40 minutes, until the lentils are tender. Serve with vermicelli that has been cooked al dente. Top with grated Parmesan or Romano cheese.

Serves 4-6

Not your usual sauce. Healthy and tasty.

Carrot and Beet Marinara Sauce

1½ cups water
6 carrots, peeled and cut into 1-inch slices
2 medium beets, peeled and cut into slices
1 large onion, quartered
1 stalk celery, sliced
4 cloves garlic, minced
1 tablespoon fresh basil, chopped
1 tablespoon fresh thyme, chopped
1 tablespoon fresh oregano, chopped
½ cup parsley, minced
12 ounces whole wheat pasta, cooked al dente
Chopped walnuts to garnish

In a sauce pan add 1½ cups of water, sliced carrots and beets. Simmer over medium heat for 15 minutes or until fork-tender. Add water as necessary. In a skillet, sauté garlic, onion, celery, basil, thyme, oregano, and parsley for 5 minutes. Place cooked garlic herb mixture and carrot/beet mixture in a food processor. Process until puréed. Serve with your favorite pasta. Garnish with chopped walnuts.

Serves 4

P
A
S
T
A

Margherita Pasta Sauce

1 28-ounce can Italian plum tomatoes, chopped and undrained
½ cup freshly chopped basil
6 tablespoons unsalted butter
½ teaspoon salt
½ teaspoon sugar
½ cup whipping cream (optional)

Heat tomatoes (with juice) and basil over medium-high heat until boiling. Use a spoon to mash the tomatoes. Reduce heat to low. Add butter, salt, and sugar. Simmer 10-12 minutes. If you like, add the cream right before serving. Toss with pasta and serve immediately.

Serves 6

This is one of the easiest and most delicious pasta sauces. It's great on any kind of flat pasta or ravioli; and according to my sister who spent a year abroad in Florence, it "tastes just like fresh Pizza Margherita in Italy" (hence the name). This also freezes well, so double the recipe!

MAIN COURSES

Contents

Platte Canyon Cowboy Steak

1 tablespoon salt
2 tablespoons sugar or sugar substitute
¼ cup pure red chili
2 tablespoons paprika
1 tablespoon garlic powder
2 tablespoons onion powder
1 tablespoon black pepper
1 tablespoon Worcestershire sauce
2 tablespoons olive oil
2 16-ounce bone-in rib-eye steaks

In a small bowl, combine all ingredients, except for the steaks, until a paste forms. Rub paste into steaks and marinate in refrigerator uncovered for 4-6 hours, or marinate at room temperature for 1 hour, uncovered. Turn steaks often so that both sides are exposed to the air. Prepare grill if cooking outside, or prepare griddle pan if cooking indoors. Place steaks on grill and cook over high heat, 4-6 minutes per side, until steaks reach desired degree of doneness. Allow to rest for 3 minutes before serving.

Serves 2

These steaks go well with Cumin Coleslaw.

Pure red chili can be found in cellophane packages in the Mexican food aisle.

103

Aidell's Spice Rub for Beef and Pork

1 tablespoon Hungarian paprika
1 tablespoon chili powder
½-1 teaspoon cayenne pepper
1 tablespoon granulated garlic or garlic powder
1 tablespoon light or dark brown sugar
½ tablespoon ground cumin
½ tablespoon dry mustard powder
½ teaspoon ground sage
½ teaspoon dried oregano
2 tablespoons kosher salt
½ tablespoon fresh ground black pepper

Mix all ingredients together. Rub into meat — great for ribs, chops, steaks, etc. For best results let meat marinate for 2 hours at room temperature or overnight in refrigerator.

Makes enough for 1-2 slabs of ribs.

Steak with Spinach and Blue Cheese

2   large cloves garlic, chopped
1   teaspoon salt
¼   teaspoon pepper
1   2-pound boneless sirloin steak (about 1½-1¾-inch thick)
1½   teaspoons olive oil or canola oil
1   tablespoon butter
2   10-ounce bags spinach leaves, triple-washed
4   ounces high quality blue cheese, crumbled

Preheat oven to 425°F. Chop the garlic, salt, and pepper together on a board until a paste forms. Rub paste evenly on both sides of steak. Heat oil in a large ovenproof skillet over high heat. Add steak and cook 3 minutes per side, until deeply browned. Transfer to oven and roast 15-20 minutes for medium-rare or longer for more doneness. Let stand 10 minutes, then slice into ½-inch pieces.

During stand time, melt butter in a large saucepan over medium heat. Add spinach and cover with a tight-fitting lid. Cook 1 minute, until spinach wilts. Add cheese and stir to melt. Divide spinach on plates. Cut steak into ½-inch thick slices. Lay slices over spinach and drizzle with drippings.

Serves 4

M
A
I
N

C
O
U
R
S
E
S

Flank Steak with Rosemary and Sage

2   tablespoons fresh rosemary leaves, finely chopped
3   tablespoons fresh sage, finely chopped
2½   teaspoons extra virgin olive oil
½   teaspoon seasoned salt
½   teaspoon garlic pepper seasoning
2   cloves garlic, minced
1   2½-pound flank steak

Blend rosemary, sage, olive oil, seasoned salt, garlic pepper, and minced garlic in a small bowl. Spread mixture evenly on both sides of the steak and press in lightly. Chill for 1 hour. Remove from refrigerator and bring to room temperature before grilling.

Preheat grill and then grill steak 6-9 minutes on each side or to desired degree of doneness. Slice steak across grain into thin slices and serve.

Serves 4

Mary Carol's Roast Tenderloin

1	4-5-pound beef tenderloin, trimmed
	Olive oil
	Cracked black peppercorns
	Garlic powder
2-4	cloves garlic, peeled and thinly sliced

Preheat oven to 425°F. Coat beef generously with olive oil and roll in cracked black pepper. Sprinkle liberally with garlic powder. Tuck slender tips of tenderloin underneath to create uniform thickness. Place on pan in oven, uncovered, for 15-20 minutes (20-25 minutes for high altitude). Remove beef from oven and pat sliced garlic on top of tenderloin. Return to oven and roast another 10-15 minutes or until desired doneness. Remove from oven and allow to rest at least 5-10 minutes before slicing.

Serves 10-12

This tenderloin can be wrapped in plastic and refrigerated for up to two days before serving. Allow tenderloin to return to room temperature before cooking.

Carbonnade de Bœuf à la Flamande

Beef Braised in Beer, Belgian Style

2	large onions, sliced
1¼	pounds stewing beef
1	ounce butter
2	tablespoons olive oil
1	ounce flour
	Salt and freshly ground black pepper
2	ounces lean bacon
1	8-ounce ale, or any good dark beer
8	fluid ounces beef stock
1	teaspoon mustard
2	teaspoons sugar
	Bouquet garni (bay leaf, 2-3 parsley sprigs, a sprig or two of thyme, tied together with string)
12	prunes, pitted

Cut onions into thin slices and the meat into strips. In a Dutch oven, fry onions in hot butter and oil until golden brown. Remove and set aside. Coat the meat in flour seasoned with salt and pepper and fry for several minutes until well browned. Add remaining ingredients, bring to a boil, stirring well to release the glaze from the pan, and make a smooth sauce. Cook for 1-2 hours at 325-350°F, or lower the heat, cover the pan tightly, and cook for approximately the same time.

Serves 4-6

Colorado Beef Brisket with Homemade Barbecue Sauce

BRISKET

1   3-pound beef brisket
2   cloves garlic, crushed
1   tablespoon chili powder
1   teaspoon paprika
1   teaspoon ground cumin
¾   teaspoon ground sage
½   teaspoon oregano
½   teaspoon sugar
¼   teaspoon freshly ground
     pepper

BARBECUE SAUCE

1   medium onion, sliced
2   tablespoons olive oil
¼   cup cider vinegar
½   cup reserved pan juices
½   cup ketchup
½   cup chili sauce
1   tablespoon soy sauce
1   tablespoon Worcestershire
     sauce
2   tablespoons brown sugar
2   teaspoons dry mustard
¼   teaspoon black pepper
     Salt and cayenne pepper to
     taste

Preheat oven to 250°F. Rub garlic into brisket on both sides. In a small bowl, mix all remaining ingredients. Rub the brisket with the spice mixture. Wrap it tightly in heavy-duty tinfoil, double-sealing edges. Place the brisket in a shallow pan and roast for 6 hours. Remove from oven and let cool. When it is thoroughly cooled, unwrap meat and reserve pan juices. Slice beef very thinly with sharp knife. Beef can be served cold or heated with reserved juices. It can also be served on rolls with a barbecue sauce mixed with the juices.

To make the Barbecue Sauce, in a medium-sized pan, sauté onion in olive oil. Add remaining ingredients and simmer until sauce reaches desired thickness.

Serves 6-8

Beef brisket is a lean flavorful meat and the long, slow cooking with spices makes it very tender. It is also a good make-ahead meal as it can be prepared 2 days in advance of serving. Excellent on a hot summer day with potato salad!

106

M A I N

C O U R S E S

Let a roast — beef, pork, lamb or poultry — sit about
5 to 10 minutes before carving. This will allow the juices
to redistribute into the meat. If a roast is carved too
soon, much of the flavor of the juices will be lost.

Waltraud's Bavarian Rouladen

2 ¼-inch thick round steaks, or 4-6 breakfast steaks
Spicy mustard
1 sour pickle, sliced into long strips
2-3 slices bacon
¼ onion, minced
¼ onion, sliced into long strips
1 carrot, minced
1 stalk celery, minced
2 tablespoons olive oil
2 tablespoons butter
1-2 tablespoons flour
1 cup water
1 beef bouillon cube
Salt and pepper to taste
Toothpicks or cooking string

Smear meat with mustard and sprinkle with salt and pepper. Put sliced pickle, bacon, and minced onions on each steak. Roll up meat and skewer with toothpicks, or tie with cooking string. Over medium-high heat in a large sauté pan, heat olive oil and butter until bubbling. Add meat and brown on all sides. Remove and keep warm. In the same pan, brown the strips of onions, minced carrot, and celery. Add 1-2 tablespoons flour and stir into vegetables until coated. Add water and beef bouillon, stirring until the cube is dissolved. Return meat to the pan, cover with a lid, and simmer 45 minutes. Add more water as needed during cooking. Once the meat is cooked, remove the meat to a warm platter. Add a little salt and pepper to the gravy and pour the gravy over the meat. Serve immediately.

Serves 4

My mother came to the United States from Germany in November of 1951. She is a terrific cook and baker of fruit flans and tortes. For a special treat she sends away for German seeds that produce a salad green known as Rapunzel, Acker Salat, Sonnen Werbele, or Feld Salat. For a 100-percent German meal, serve this dish with the Sonnen Werbele, Späetzle, and Brussels sprouts and then a fruit flan for dessert.

MAIN COURSES

Chateaubriand with Béarnaise Sauce

BÉARNAISE SAUCE

2	tablespoons green shallots, finely minced
¼	teaspoon garlic, finely minced
2	teaspoons freshly squeezed lemon juice
¼	cup dry white wine
½	tablespoon dried chervil
½	tablespoon dried tarragon
⅛	teaspoon salt
¼	teaspoon freshly ground pepper
½	cup salted butter
3	large egg yolks
½	cup salted butter
	Pinch of red pepper

TENDERLOIN

1	1½-2-pound center-cut beef tenderloin, prime grade
3	tablespoons butter
2	cloves garlic, mashed
	Salt and pepper

Béarnaise sauce: In a small saucepan combine shallots, garlic, lemon juice, wine, chervil, tarragon, salt, and pepper. Cook over medium heat until the mixture is reduced to about 2 tablespoons. Place egg yolks and red pepper in blender, cover, and blend on high speed for a few seconds, just to break the yolks. Add the glaze, cover again, and turn on high speed for a few seconds more. In separate saucepan, melt butter. Remove the blender cover, turn on high speed, and gradually pour in the hot melted butter in a steady stream. Cover the blender and switch on for 60 seconds and then off 30 seconds. Repeat the on-off procedure until the sauce thickens. Set aside and keep warm until ready to serve. This sauce can be easily doubled.

Tenderloin: Preheat grill. Melt butter with 2 mashed garlic cloves. Coat the surface of meat and season with salt and pepper. Place tenderloin on hot grill and sear on each side for about 4 minutes. Reduce heat and continue grilling until it reaches the desired doneness. Roasting time will vary depending on the diameter of the meat. To be certain of the doneness that you desire, use an instant-read thermometer. Remove from grill and transfer to a cutting board. Spoon about 3 tablespoons of Béarnaise sauce onto the center of warm plates. Carve the tenderloin into ½-inch diagonal slices. Place onto the Béarnaise sauce. Put the remainder of the sauce in a container on the table.

Serves 2-4, depending on the size of tenderloin

Allow 8 ounces per person.

A local meat market should be able to prepare the tenderloin for you. If not, trim tenderloin of unnecessary fat. The tenderloin should be about 1-inch thick, but if it's too thick, pound it to flatten.

A 19th-century French author, François Châteaubriand, invented this dish. To make a perfect romantic dinner for two, use a 1-pound tenderloin. Add roasted potatoes and a fresh green salad. French Burgundy is a wonderful red wine to enhance the flavors of this meal.

109

Spicy Beef with Snow Peas

1	pound lean tender beef, sliced very thin
1	tablespoon soy sauce
1	tablespoon cornstarch
1	tablespoon water
1	tablespoon vegetable oil
1	cup vegetable oil
¼	pound snow peas
	Pepper to taste
1	teaspoon Asian chili paste

For marinade, mix the soy sauce, cornstarch, water, and 1 tablespoon vegetable oil. Marinate beef slices for 1 hour.

Preheat wok or heavy skillet. Pour in ¾ cup vegetable oil. When oil is hot, add beef and stir to separate pieces, so each piece gets cooked in a short time. Transfer to a plate. Use the remaining oil to stir-fry the snow peas briefly. Return beef to wok or skillet with the snow peas. Add pepper and stir to mix. Add chili paste and stir. Serve warm.

Serves 2-4

In 1978 this authentic recipe was given to me by a Chinese snow pea farmer in Corvallis, Oregon. No kidding! Even after living in Taiwan, this is the recipe that remains one of our favorites. Serve it with Bean Thread Soup.

Cajun Meat Loaf

3 tablespoons unsalted butter
¾ cup finely chopped onion
½ cup finely chopped celery
½ cup puréed red bell pepper, or finely chopped
¼ cup sliced green onions
3 cloves garlic, minced
1 tablespoon hot pepper sauce
2 tablespoons Worcestershire sauce
1 tablespoon salt
1 teaspoon cayenne pepper
1 teaspoon black pepper
½ teaspoon white pepper
½ teaspoon cumin
½ teaspoon nutmeg
½ cup heavy cream, or half-and-half
½ cup ketchup
1 pound ground beef
½ pound ground pork (see note below)
½ pound ground veal (see note below)
2 eggs, beaten
1 cup breadcrumbs
   Cooking spray

Preheat oven at 350°F. In a medium saucepan, melt butter over medium heat. When it foams add onions, celery, red peppers, green onions, garlic, pepper sauce, Worcestershire sauce, salt, cayenne pepper, black pepper, white pepper, cumin, and nutmeg. Cook approximately 5 minutes, stirring often, until mixture begins to stick. Stir in cream and ketchup, lower heat, and cook an additional 5 minutes. Remove from heat and cool to room temperature.

In a large bowl, combine the meats with the onion mixture, eggs, and breadcrumbs. Mix thoroughly. It might look and feel "wet" but that's okay. Transfer to an ovenproof glass loaf pan that has been sprayed with cooking spray. Bake uncovered for 25 minutes. Raise temperature to 400°F and bake for 35 minutes longer, or until meat thermometer reads 160°F.

Serves 4-6

The grocery store might not have already ground pork or ground veal but will grind it for you.

Place a strip of bacon in bottom
of meat loaf pan to prevent sticking.

Pork with Olives and Capers

1 pound pork tenderloins or cutlets
  Salt and pepper
¼ cup flour
1 tablespoon olive oil
½ cup white wine
½ cup chicken broth
½ cup chopped Kalamata olives
2 tablespoons capers
2 tablespoons chopped Italian parsley

Cut pork if necessary and pound to ¼-inch pieces. Sprinkle both sides with salt and pepper and dredge in flour. Heat half of olive oil in a heavy skillet over medium-high heat. Brown pork for 2 minutes per side. Repeat until all pork is browned, using remaining olive oil as needed. Remove pork and set aside. To the skillet add wine, broth, capers, and olives. Stir until mixed. Return pork to skillet and cook about 4 minutes. Sprinkle with parsley and serve immediately.

Serves 4

Vance's Pork Tenderloin

PORK
1 1½-pound pork tenderloin

DRY RUB
  Garlic powder to taste
1 teaspoon medium ground black pepper
1 teaspoon white pepper
1 teaspoon ground dry mustard

MARINADE
⅓ cup olive oil
1 tablespoon soy sauce
1 tablespoon Worcestershire sauce
  Cajun seasoning

To make the rub, in a small bowl, combine the rub ingredients. Coat tenderloin with dry rub mix. Mix marinade and place tenderloin in the marinade, turning to cover well. Marinate for ½-2 hours (no more as it will overpower the flavor of pork). Remove meat from marinade, reserving liquid. Season the tenderloin with a good Cajun seasoning. Grill on barbeque grill for 15-20 minutes or on stovetop in heavy skillet 10-15 minutes, until medium rare. Do not overcook. If the outside browns before middle is done, remove from heat, slice into 1-inch rounds, and quickly finish over heat. Pour a small amount of liquid over meat into pan and heat through for au jus gravy. Serve immediately.

Serves 4

This is great with macaroni and cheese or potatoes au gratin.

Sautéed Pork Chops with Maple Bourbon Sauce

PORK CHOPS

4   1¼-1½-inch center cut pork loin chops, either rib or T-bone, trimmed of external fat

1   tablespoon olive oil

PAN SAUCE

½   cup finely chopped onions

½   cup chicken stock

4   tablespoons Bourbon whiskey

1   tablespoon cider vinegar

1   tablespoon maple syrup

    Pinch of ground ginger and nutmeg

    Salt and freshly ground black pepper

112

Marinate the chops overnight in the refrigerator using Aidell's Spice Rub. It really makes a fantastic contribution to the finished dish. Let the refrigerated meat come to room temperature before cooking.

In a large heavy skillet, heat the oil over high heat. When the pan is hot enough to sear the chops but not burn them, add the chops. They should make a gentle hissing sound when they hit the pan, not an explosive splutter. Adjust the heat if the pan seems too hot, or remove the pan from the heat for about 30 seconds. Sear chops on one side for 1-2 minutes, or until beginning to brown lightly. Turn chops over and sear for one more minute.

Reduce heat so that the chops continue to sizzle. If the heat is too low, the chops will sweat and juices will exude from the meat and leave it dry. Cover the pan and cook for 3-4 minutes, depending on how thick the chops are. Turn and cook them for 3-4 minutes more on the other side. The chops are done when the meat is firm but not hard when pressed with a finger. For the juiciest chops, remove from the pan when an inserted meat thermometer registers 145°F. Cover loosely with foil and let them rest for about 5 minutes before serving, to stabilize the juices. After resting the thermometer should read 150°F.

To make the pan sauce, pour off all but 1 tablespoon of the fat and add the onions. Cook for 3 minutes, covered, over medium heat, stirring occasionally. Stir in the stock, Bourbon, vinegar, syrup, and spices, scraping up any browned bits from the bottom of the pan. Boil the sauce for 2-3 minutes. It should not become syrupy, but will have an intense flavor nonetheless. Taste for salt and pepper. Pour the sauce over the chops and serve. Also tastes great served with new potatoes and wilted spinach.

Serves 4

The sauce is also excellent with grilled pork chops, smoked pork chops, ham steaks, and brined pork chops.

Fruit-Glazed Pork over Mixed Greens

4	12-ounce pork tenderloins
1¼	teaspoons salt
½	teaspoon freshly ground pepper
5	tablespoons olive oil, divided
⅓	cup no-sugar-added orange marmalade
⅓	cup no-sugar-added apricot jam
½	teaspoon ground cinnamon
1	tablespoon plus 1½ teaspoons balsamic vinegar
1	clove garlic, minced
6	cups (5 ounces) mixed greens

113

Preheat oven to 400°F. Season pork with salt and pepper. In a large skillet over medium-high heat, warm 1 tablespoon of oil. Brown pork for about 10 minutes, turning as needed. Transfer to a rimmed baking sheet and place in oven. Roast pork for 10 minutes.

Meanwhile, in a small bowl, whisk together orange marmalade, apricot jam, and cinnamon. Transfer 1 tablespoon of the jam mixture to a large bowl and set aside.

Brush pork with jam mixture. Cook 5 more minutes, or until just cooked through and a meat thermometer registers 160°F. Transfer pork to a cutting board and let stand for 5 minutes before cutting into 1-inch diagonal slices.

Whisk vinegar, garlic, and remaining oil into reserved jam mixture; add greens and toss to coat. Divide greens on plates and top with pork slices and any accumulated juices.

Serves 6

If you can't find marmalade without added sugar, simply use more apricot jam.

MAIN COURSES

Sweet and Sour Sauce for Leftover Pork

1	small onion
1	medium green pepper
1	small celery heart
5	slices canned pineapple
½	cup water
¾	cup white vinegar
1	cup sugar
2	tablespoons ketchup
1	teaspoon soy sauce
4	tablespoons cornstarch
⅓	cup pineapple juice
	Left over pork, cut into bite-sized pieces
	Cooked rice

Cut onion in half crosswise and then in chunks about ¾-inch wide. Cut pepper into chunks. Cut celery on the diagonal, ½-inch thick. Cut pineapple into chunks.

Heat a large skillet. Pour ¼ cup water, vinegar, sugar, ketchup, and soy sauce into pan and bring to a boil. Mix remaining water with cornstarch. Stir cornstarch mixture into sauce and cook for 2 minutes. Add vegetables and cook until peppers turn brilliant green. Add pineapple juice and pineapple pieces. If the sauce is too thick, add more pineapple juice.

If making Sweet and Sour Pork, add the cooked meat with the vegetables to heat through. Serve over rice.

Serves 4

Pulled Pork Barbecue with Hot Pepper Vinegar Sauce

RUB MIX

1	tablespoon paprika
1	tablespoon firmly packed light brown sugar
1½	teaspoons chili powder
1½	teaspoons ground cumin
1	teaspoon coarsely ground black pepper
1	teaspoon kosher salt
½	teaspoon cayenne pepper
1	4-5-pound boneless pork shoulder roast (Boston butt), rolled and tied

HOT PEPPER VINEGAR SAUCE

1½	cups cider vinegar
2	tablespoons granulated sugar
1	teaspoon hot pepper sauce
½	teaspoon crushed red pepper flakes
	Kosher salt
	Freshly ground black pepper
	Hamburger buns

To make the rub, in a small bowl, combine the rub ingredients. Coat the roast evenly with the rub. Allow standing at room temperature for 30 minutes before grilling.

Grill the roast, fat side up, not directly over the coals, until the internal temperature reaches 160°F, 3-4 hours. The meat should be so tender it pulls apart easily. Remove from the grill, place on a platter, and loosely cover with foil. Allow resting for about 20 minutes.

To make the sauce, in a medium-sized saucepan combine the sauce ingredients, including salt and pepper to taste, and bring to a boil. Reduce heat to low and simmer for 10 minutes. Keep warm.

Thinly slice, chop, or "pull" the pork meat into shreds with your fingers or two forks, discarding any large bits of fat. Moisten the meat with some of the sauce and mix well in a bowl. Grill the buns until lightly toasted about 30 seconds. Serve the pulled pork warm on the buns with the remaining sauce on the side.

Makes 12-15 sandwiches.

Red Beans and Rice
with Andouille Sausage

1   package dried pinto or
       Anasazi beans
1   can beef broth
1   medium onion, finely chopped
2   ribs celery, finely chopped
2   bay leaves
1   teaspoon Worcestershire sauce
1   teaspoon marjoram
1   teaspoon ground cumin
1   teaspoon chili powder
½   teaspoon ground thyme
½   teaspoon crushed red pepper
1½   teaspoons salt
1   can tomato sauce
1   can diced tomatoes
1   carrot, sliced (optional)
1   pound lean ground beef
1   pound andouille sausage
       (cut into ½-inch slices)
      Cooked white rice
      Cornbread

M A I N   C O U R S E S

Rinse beans and soak overnight or at least 3-4 hours. Place beans in heavy stockpot with warm water and beef broth, just enough to cover beans. Bring to boil. Add onions, celery, bay leaves, Worcestershire sauce, marjoram, cumin, chili powder, thyme, red pepper, and salt. Return to boil, reduce heat to simmer, cover and cook for 1 hour, add water as needed. Add tomato sauce, tomatoes, and carrot slices, continue cooking.

In a medium-sized skillet brown ground meat and drain well. Slice sausage and add both meats to beans. For about 30 minutes more, cook until beans are tender and are just beginning to separate. Here is where the altitude is of importance - you might actually have to cook this up to a couple of hours more. Just keep adding water and/or beef broth as needed. Remove 1 cup of beans, purée or mash with a spoon, and add back to pot to thicken the broth. Remove bay leaves and carrots. You may add more chili powder to taste. Serve over white rice with cornbread.

Serves 6-8

You may want to increase the amount of sausage used depending on the prevalence of "sausage stealers" in your family. Take note, however, that in order to deter the sausage thieves, you can't put all the sausage in at once! Otherwise, you'll just create such a bounty that they'll pilfer even more. Instead, put in half of it and let people start serving themselves. Then come back and add the rest.

Red beans and rice is, to a large extent, a fix-it-and-forget-it dish. In the South it was traditionally served on Mondays (washing day) because one could put it on the stove to cook in the morning and leave it all day. Opinions vary greatly regarding the proper "soupiness" of the red bean broth. Some cooks prefer to let most of the water cook down, leaving a very thick mixture. Others tend to retain enough liquid so that the beans and sausage are still floating around. This is strictly a matter of preference, and you can experiment to find the right consistency for you. If your dish is getting too thick, just add additional water or beef broth and continue cooking.

117

M A I N   C O U R S E S

Sweet Italian Sausage with Mediterranean Vegetables

2   tablespoons olive oil

8   ounces sweet Italian sausage, casings removed

1   cup diced (½-inch pieces) eggplant

1   cup diced (½-inch pieces) zucchini

1   cup diced (½-inch pieces) red bell pepper

½   cup chopped onion

2   cloves garlic, minced

1   28-ounce can Italian plum tomatoes, drained and chopped

2   tablespoons chopped fresh parsley

2   tablespoons chopped fresh basil leaves

     Cayenne or black pepper to taste

2   ounces grated mozzarella cheese

Preheat oven to 350°F. In a sauté pan, brown the sausage meat in olive oil for about 10 minutes, breaking up the meat with a spoon. With a slotted spoon, remove browned meat to a bowl, reserve. To the same pot, add the eggplant, zucchini, bell pepper, onion, and garlic. Stirring occasionally, cook until softened, about 10-15 minutes. Stir in the reserved sausage, tomatoes, parsley, basil, and cayenne pepper. Reduce the heat and simmer for 15 minutes. Spoon the mixture into an 8x9-inch oven-to-table baking dish and sprinkle with the mozzarella cheese. Bake until cheese melts, about 15 minutes.

Serves 4

Colorado Chicken Mole — A Traditional Mexican Dish

4   skinless chicken breasts
     Juice from 2 limes
1   teaspoon garlic powder
     Salt and pepper
3   medium tomatoes, seeded and
       chopped, or 1 12-ounce can
       diced tomatoes
½   cup ground toasted almonds
2   poblano peppers, roasted,
       seeded, and chopped
2   cloves garlic, thinly sliced
2   tablespoons finely chopped
       yellow onions
½   teaspoon chopped cilantro plus
       sprigs for garnish
½   teaspoon ground cayenne
       pepper
     Salt to taste
3   tablespoons Dutch cocoa
       powder
⅛   teaspoon ground cinnamon
1   tablespoon butter, melted
2   tablespoons top shelf tequila
1   12-ounce can chicken broth, or
       2 cups fresh broth
3   tablespoons olive oil
1   teaspoon cornstarch, if needed
     Cooked rice
     Fresh chopped tomatoes and
       avocado slices for garnish
     Sea salt and fresh ground
       pepper

Season breasts with lime juice. Rub garlic powder, salt, and pepper into chicken and set aside.

To prepare sauce mixture purée tomatoes, almonds, peppers, garlic, onions, and cilantro in food processor or blender in short bursts. Add cayenne pepper, salt, cocoa powder, cinnamon, butter, tequila, and 1 cup of chicken broth. Blend well. The sauce should have the consistency of tomato sauce; it should pour easily.

Transfer sauce to 12-inch nonstick sauté pan and simmer over low heat, uncovered. Cook for about 30 minutes, stirring occasionally. Don't let sauce thicken too much as it will scorch. Stir in additional broth for thinning. Mix a little chicken broth with cornstarch and stir into mixture if too thin.

While sauce is cooking, in a medium-sized skillet, cook chicken breasts in olive oil, or rub breast with olive oil and broil in oven. Chicken should be brown on both sides. When browned, remove from heat and place in skillet with sauce. Ladle sauce over chicken, cover, and simmer for about 20 minutes, or until chicken is tender and thoroughly cooked. Check while cooking, ladling sauce and stirring, so sauce doesn't scorch.

Serve over cooked rice. Garnish with sprigs of cilantro, fresh chopped tomatoes, and avocados slices. Sprinkle with a little sea salt and ground pepper if desired.

Serves 4

It is necessary to use pure Dutch cocoa, available from specialty markets.

Monterey Chicken

8	boneless chicken breasts, skinned
½	cup breadcrumbs
¼	cup Parmesan cheese, grated
3	teaspoons chili powder
½	teaspoon salt
¼	teaspoon pepper
¼	teaspoon cumin
½	pound Monterey Jack cheese, cut into strips
1	7-ounce can diced green chilies
1	stick butter, melted
⅓	cup sliced green onions (optional)
	Sour cream (optional)

SAUCE
1	15-ounce can tomato sauce
½	teaspoon ground cumin

Preheat oven to 400°F. Pound chicken breast thin. Combine the next 6 ingredients in a bowl. Place strip of cheese and one tablespoon of green chilies on each chicken breast, roll up, secure with toothpicks, dredge in butter, and roll in the dry ingredients. Drizzle any remaining butter over chicken. Bake uncovered in oven for 25-35 minutes (longer if made ahead and refrigerated).

Heat tomato sauce and cumin in a saucepan just before serving.

Garnish with sauce, sour cream, and green onions.

Serves 8

Caribbean Jerk Chicken

2	cups scallions
2	jalapeño or habanero peppers, seeded
2	tablespoons soy sauce
2	tablespoons lime juice
5	teaspoons allspice
3	teaspoons dry mustard
2	bay leaves
2	cloves garlic
1	tablespoon salt
2	teaspoons sugar
1½	teaspoons dried thyme
1	teaspoon cinnamon
5	pounds chicken (breast, strips, or cubes for kabobs)

In a food processor or blender, process all ingredients (except chicken) to make a marinade. Place chicken in a bag or pan and add marinade. Marinate 24-72 hours. Turn over pieces of chicken every few hours. Cook on a hot grill, until cooked through.

Serves 10 (as a main course or up to 20 as appetizers)

The longer the meat marinates, the more it yields a moist and flavorful result. The cubes or strips make great skewered appetizers. This is a fantastic make-ahead dish.

Cajun Jambalaya

CREOLE SEASONING
2½	tablespoons paprika
2	tablespoons salt
2	tablespoons garlic powder
1	tablespoon black pepper
1	tablespoon onion powder
1	tablespoon cayenne pepper
1	tablespoon oregano
1	tablespoon dried thyme

JAMBALAYA
12	medium shrimp, peeled, deveined, and chopped
4	ounces chicken, diced
1	tablespoon Creole seasoning
2	tablespoons olive oil
¼	onion, chopped
¼	cup chopped green bell pepper
¼	cup chopped celery
2	tablespoons chopped garlic
½	cup diced tomatoes (you may use canned tomatoes)
3	bay leaves
1	teaspoon Worcestershire sauce
1	teaspoon hot sauce
¾	cup rice
3	cups chicken broth
5	ounces andouille sausage, sliced into ½-inch pieces
	Salt and pepper

To make the Creole seasoning, combine all seasoning ingredients thoroughly. Makes ⅔ cup.

In a bowl combine shrimp, chicken, and 1 tablespoon Creole seasoning and work in seasoning well. In a large Dutch oven or heavy pot, heat oil over high heat with onions, peppers, and celery for 3 minutes. Add garlic, tomatoes, bay leaves, Worcestershire sauce, and hot sauce. Stir in rice and slowly add chicken broth. When rice is just tender, add shrimp and chicken mixture, and the sausage. Cook until meat is done, about 10 minutes or less. Season to taste with salt, pepper, and Creole seasoning.

Serves 4

For a healthier dish you may prefer to use Basmati or brown rice. This dish was made with brown rice at 9,000 feet. It took about 45 minutes for the rice cook. It takes about 25 minutes for white rice to cook. You can find andouille sausage at specialty meat markets.

MAIN COURSES

Curried Yogurt Chicken

1	teaspoon ground cumin
2	teaspoons garam masala
1	teaspoon ground coriander
1	teaspoon black pepper
½	teaspoon dried basil
½	teaspoon fennel seeds
2	teaspoons dried parsley
1	teaspoon garlic powder or 3 cloves fresh garlic, minced
1	teaspoon onion powder
1	tablespoon soy sauce or tamari
2	tablespoons maple syrup
	Juice of 1 lemon
2	cups plain yogurt
2-2½	pounds jumbo chicken tenders

Mix spices, soy sauce, syrup, and lemon juice into the plain yogurt. Cover the chicken with yogurt mixture and let marinate in the refrigerator for at least 4 hours, or overnight is fine.

Preheat over to 450°F. Spread some of the marinade in a baking dish and place chicken on top. Let bake for 5 minutes, reduce heat to 350°F, and cook another 15-20 minutes until done. Baste with remaining yogurt mixture as needed.

Serves 6-10

This recipe is great with mashed potatoes. For appetizers, cut into bite-size pieces and skewer with toothpicks. Makes great left overs and can be eaten cold.

Balti Butter Chicken

5	fluid ounces natural yogurt
2	ounces ground almonds
1½	teaspoons chili powder
¼	teaspoon crushed bay leaves
¼	teaspoon ground cloves
¼	teaspoon ground cinnamon
1	teaspoon garam masala
4	green cardamom pods
1	teaspoon ginger pulp
1	teaspoon garlic pulp
1	14-ounce can tomatoes
1¼	teaspoons salt
2	pounds skinless chicken, boned and cubed
3	ounces butter
1	tablespoon corn oil
2	medium onions, sliced
2	tablespoons fresh cilantro, chopped
4	tablespoons light cream

Place yogurt, ground almonds, all dry spices, ginger, garlic, tomatoes, and salt in a mixing bowl and blend together thoroughly. Put chicken in a bowl and cover with yogurt mixture; set aside.

Melt together butter and oil in a medium karahi, wok, or frying pan. Add onions and sauté for about 3 minutes. Add chicken mixture and stir-fry for about 7-10 minutes. Stir in half the cilantro and mix well. Pour in cream, stir well, and bring liquid to a boil. Serve garnished with the remaining chopped cilantro.

Serves 4

Lemon Barbeque Chicken

1   cup vegetable oil
½   cup fresh squeezed lemon juice
1   tablespoon salt
1   teaspoon paprika
2   teaspoons onion powder
2   teaspoons dried basil
½   teaspoon thyme
½   teaspoon garlic powder
2   broiler fryer chickens with skin,
      cut into pieces

In a medium bowl, blend together oil, lemon juice, salt, paprika, onion powder, sweet basil, thyme, and garlic powder. Place chicken in a shallow 9x13-inch glass dish or large plastic container with lid. Pour marinade over chicken; cover tightly and marinate in refrigerator 6-8 hours or overnight, turning occasionally. Remove chicken from refrigerator 1 hour before grilling. Preheat grill on high, place chicken on hot grill, skin side up, turn heat down to medium. Brush with marinade. Watch carefully and turn often. Cook until done. Serve with rice flavored with chicken broth and lemon.

Serves 6 to 8

After marinating chicken can baked in 350°F oven for 45-60 minutes or until done. This dish may also be made with turkey pieces.

Try replacing herbs and spices in recipes with a different herb or spice. Use marjoram instead of oregano, savory instead of thyme, cilantro instead of parsley, anise seed instead of fennel, etc.

Lemon Thyme Chicken

3 tablespoons flour
½ teaspoon salt
¼ teaspoon pepper
4 chicken breast halves, boneless
    and skinless
2 tablespoons oil
1 medium onion, chopped
1 tablespoon butter or margarine
1 cup chicken broth
3 tablespoons lemon juice,
    freshly squeezed
½ teaspoon dried thyme
2 tablespoons fresh parsley,
    chopped for garnish
    Lemon wedges for garnish

Combine flour, salt, and pepper in a plastic bag and shake to mix. Add chicken and shake to lightly coat. Remove chicken and reserve flour.

Warm 1 tablespoon oil in a large skillet on medium heat, add chicken, and brown on one side, about 5-7 minutes. Add the remaining 1 tablespoon of oil, turn chicken, and brown well on the second side, 5-7 minutes more. Transfer chicken to plate and set aside.

Add butter to skillet, melt, then add chopped onions and cook until softened. Stir in reserved seasoned flour and cook, stirring until flour is completely incorporated, 1-2 minutes.

Add broth, 2 tablespoons of the lemon juice and thyme. Bring mixture to a boil stirring constantly. Return chicken to the skillet. Reduce heat to medium-low and cover. Simmer until chicken is completely cooked, 5-10 minutes.

To serve, divide chicken among 4 plates. Stir remaining tablespoon of lemon juice into sauce and pour over chicken, and garnish with chopped parsley and lemon wedges. More lemon may be added depending on taste preference.

Serves 4

This simple dish is heart-healthy.

Serve with steamed broccoli and rice flavored with chicken broth.

123

M
A
I
N

C
O
U
R
S
E
S

Emmentaler Chicken with Broccoli Florets

4 cups broccoli florets, steamed and drained, set aside in large bowl

4 tablespoons butter

¾ pound mushrooms, sliced

1 small onion, diced

1 14-ounce can artichoke hearts, rinsed, drained, and cut into bite-size pieces

5 tablespoons flour

2¾ cups chicken broth

1½ teaspoons Dijon mustard

½ teaspoon tarragon

½ teaspoon salt

½ teaspoon black pepper

1 cup (4 ounces) Emmentaler cheese, grated

2 pounds cooked chicken breasts, cut into bite-size pieces

¼ cup Asiago cheese, grated (optional)

Cooking spray

Preheat oven to 350°F. Prepare a 4-quart baking dish with cooking spray and set aside. In a large skillet, sauté mushrooms and onions in 1 tablespoon of butter over medium heat until mushrooms are soft and onions are translucent about 4-5 minutes. Remove from heat. Add mushrooms, onions, and artichoke hearts to broccoli. Stir to mix. Melt remaining 3 tablespoons butter (you can use the same pan you used to sauté earlier). Using a whisk, blend in flour to make a roux. Slowly add chicken broth, mustard, and seasonings, whisking until sauce is smooth and thickens about 2-3 minutes. Remove from heat and add Emmentaler cheese, stirring until smooth.

Beginning with chicken, alternatively layer chicken and vegetables in prepared baking dish. Pour cheese sauce evenly over the top of the ingredients, cover with foil, and bake 35-40 minutes. Remove foil and sprinkle top with Asiago cheese. Bake an additional 5-10 minutes, or until cheese is light to golden brown. This dish will be very hot. Let it cool a bit before serving.

Serves 8

Instead of using chicken broth, you may use reduced-salt chicken broth and dry white wine. You can increase the amount of mushrooms to 1 pound.

124

Gussie's Chicken Prosciutto

4	boneless chicken breasts
4	small slices Swiss cheese
4	thin slices Prosciutto ham
	Toothpicks
1	stick butter
	Flour
¾	cup white wine
1½	cups heavy cream
2	tablespoons soy sauce
3	tablespoons Romano cheese
	Parsley

Remove skin from chicken breast and pound with a mallet until evenly flat. Place cheese and ham on the flattened chicken and roll up. Secure with toothpicks and lightly dust in flour. In a sauté pan, melt butter and sauté chicken seam-side down for 4 minutes on each side until brown. Remove chicken and set aside. Deglaze pan with wine. Reduce liquid by ½. Add the chicken breasts back to pan and add cream and soy sauce. Sprinkle with Romano cheese and garnish with parsley. Great when served with mashed potatoes, Fettuccine Alfredo, or baked potatoes.

Serves 4

You can bake the chicken for 15 minutes at 350°F after browning it in the sauté pan. You can also season the chicken with flour before cooking, for a crisper skin.

125

For juicier meats, do not cut into the meat to check for doneness during cooking. Also, do not press or flatten meat with a spatula during cooking.

Chicken Cacciatore with Oven-Roasted Vegetables

1½ pounds Roma tomatoes, seeded and quartered length-wise

½ pound Crimini mushrooms, washed and quartered

1 large onion, cut length-wise into strips

5 tablespoons olive oil, divided

2 tablespoons sherry vinegar

Kosher salt

Freshly ground black pepper

4½ pounds chicken thighs, with bones and skin on

1½ tablespoons fresh rosemary, chopped and divided

½ cup red wine

1 14½-ounce can diced tomatoes in juice

1 cup low-salt chicken broth

½ tablespoon fresh rosemary, chopped

½ cup Chiffonade of fresh basil, divided

2 tablespoons capers, drained and divided

Preheat oven to 400°F. Combine tomatoes, mushrooms, and onions on a rimmed baking sheet and sprinkle with 3 tablespoons olive oil, vinegar, and a liberal portion of kosher salt and fresh ground black pepper. Toss to coat evenly and spread into a single layer. Roast for about 1½ hours, stirring every 15 minutes until all vegetables are tender and develop a rich caramel brown color. Remove from oven, transfer to a bowl, and set aside to cool.

Reduce oven temperature to 350°F. Season chicken with salt, freshly ground pepper, and 1 tablespoon of fresh rosemary. Heat 2 tablespoons olive oil in a large braising pan over medium-high heat. Sauté chicken until golden brown, about 7 minutes per side. Remove chicken to a bowl to allow it to rest. Deglaze pan with wine, scraping up the bits from the sauté. Reduce wine by one half. Add tomatoes with juice and chicken broth. Bring to a boil, reduce heat to medium and simmer 10 minutes to allow the flavors to meld.

Return chicken to braising pan and place in the oven. Roast uncovered for 25 minutes, or until chicken is thoroughly cooked. Meat will be firm to the touch and juices will run clear when pierced with a knife. Remove from oven and stir in roasted vegetables, ½ tablespoon rosemary, ¼ cup basil, and 1 tablespoon capers. Simmer over medium heat until the vegetables come back up to temperature. Taste for seasoning and adjust with kosher salt and fresh ground black pepper. Transfer to serving bowl and garnish with reserved basil and capers.

Serves 6

Brick-Roasted Chicken

1   3-4 pound boneless chicken (fryer) or 2 large boneless breasts

2½   tablespoons fresh thyme leaves, roughly chopped

2   tablespoons fresh rosemary, roughly chopped

6   cloves garlic, peeled and smashed

1   cup extra virgin olive oil

     Kosher salt and freshly ground black pepper

     Vegetable or olive oil, as needed

Rinse the chicken in cold water and pat dry. Combine thyme, rosemary, garlic, and olive oil in a large resealable bag or glass baking dish. Add the chicken halves or breasts. Coat both sides of chicken with marinade. Cover and refrigerate overnight or for at least 4 hours.

Heat the oven to 450°F. Wrap two bricks in a couple of layers of heavy-duty foil. (If you don't have bricks, use 2-pound weights.) Remove the chicken from the refrigerator, let the excess marinade drain off, and sprinkle with salt and pepper. Set a large cast iron or other heavy ovenproof pan over medium-high heat. When hot, add just enough vegetable oil to lightly film the pan. Place the chicken, skin side down, in the pan and immediately put a brick on top of each piece. Turn the heat to medium and cook (without moving the chicken) until the skin is a deep golden brown (check with a spatula) and the chicken is cooked about halfway through, 20-25 minutes. Remove the bricks, turn the chicken halves over, and put the pan in the hot oven to finish roasting the chicken until a thermometer registers at least 165°F, another 20-25 minutes.

Serves 2 but can be doubled to serve 4

Perhaps the best chicken you've ever tasted!

Start planning this dish a day ahead so that you can marinate it overnight.

127

Pastitsio

1   pound ground lamb, beef, or pork
½   onion, finely chopped
2   cloves garlic, minced
1   8-ounce can tomato sauce
¼   cup dry red wine
2   tablespoons snipped parsley
½   teaspoon dried oregano, crushed
¼   teaspoon salt
¼   teaspoon ground cinnamon
4   eggs, beaten individually
3   tablespoons butter
3   tablespoons all-purpose flour
¼   teaspoon black pepper
1½   cups milk plus ¼ cup milk, reserved
½   cup grated Parmesan cheese, divided
1   cup elbow macaroni, cooked and drained
    Cooking spray

Preheat oven to 350°F. In a large skillet, cook meat, onions, and garlic until meat is brown and onions are tender. Drain fat. Stir in tomato sauce, wine, parsley, oregano, salt, and cinnamon. Bring to boil. Reduce heat and simmer for 10 minutes. Gradually stir one egg into meat mixture and set aside. Cook macaroni according to package directions until al dente and drain.

In a medium saucepan melt butter and stir in flour and pepper. Add 1½ cups milk all at once. Cook and stir until thickened and bubbly. Continue cooking one more minute. Gradually stir sauce into two of beaten eggs. Add half of Parmesan cheese. Toss macaroni with remaining egg, milk, and Parmesan cheese.

To assemble, spray an 8x8-inch baking dish with cooking spray. Layer macaroni mixture, meat mixture, and all of sauce. Sprinkle with additional cinnamon if desired. Bake in oven for 30-35 minutes. Let stand for 5 minutes before serving.

Serves 6

A home-style casserole from Greece!

M A I N   C O U R S E S

Chefs pound meat not to tenderize,
but to help even the meat so it cooks evenly.

Lamb Burgers with Cucumber Dill Sauce

CUCUMBER DILL SAUCE
¼   cup chopped cucumbers
¼   cup plain yogurt
½   teaspoon chopped fresh dill
1   clove garlic, minced

BURGERS
1   10-ounce package frozen
    spinach, thawed and
    squeezed dry, or chopped
    fresh spinach
¾   pound ground lamb
1   tablespoon fresh lemon juice
½   cup crumbled feta cheese
1   egg, beaten
    (can use egg white only)
¼   teaspoon pepper
½   teaspoon salt
¼   cup chopped mint (optional)
4   hamburger buns

In a small bowl, mix together chopped cucumbers, yogurt, dill, and garlic to make the cucumber dill sauce. Chill in an airtight container for at least 30 minutes.

Prepare grill for cooking. In a large bowl, mix spinach, lamb, lemon juice, feta cheese, egg, salt, and pepper. Divide into fourths and make patties. Grill burgers to desired doneness; serve on buns with Cucumber Dill Sauce.

Serves 4

This is a favorite summer cookout meal.

Grocery stores will prepare ground lamb meat for you and it's also available frozen.

Grilled Lamb Japanese Style

1½-2   pounds 1-inch thick
       medallions of lamb, cut
       from the boneless rack or
       tenderloin
1   cup dark (red) miso
1   tablespoon minced ginger
1   teaspoon minced garlic
½   teaspoon cayenne, or to taste
      Mirin, sake or white wine as
      needed

In a large bowl, combine miso, ginger, garlic and cayenne, then thin with a little mirin or sake, to make a thick paste. Spread meat with this paste, then proceed, or cover and marinate in refrigerator for up to 24 hours.

Preheat oven to broil; rack should be 4 inches or less from heat source, or heat outdoor drill. Broil or grill meat about 4 minutes per side, until outside is crisp and inside medium-rare. Serve immediately.

Serves 4

Osso Buco

4-5 2-2½-inch thick veal shanks
½   teaspoon freshly ground black pepper
¼   teaspoon salt
1   cup flour for dredging
1   tablespoon olive oil
¾   cup dry white wine
1½   cups beef stock
1   tablespoon ground thyme
½   cup fresh basil leaves
2   bay leaves
1½   cups chopped onions
1   cup chopped celery
1   cup chopped carrots
1   tablespoon minced garlic
1   can plum tomatoes, chopped, reserving juice

GREMOLATA
½   cup finely minced flat-leaf Italian parsley
1   tablespoon grated lemon rind
1   tablespoon finely minced garlic

Preheat oven to 350°F. Salt and pepper shanks, dredge lightly in flour, and shake off excess flour. In a large pot, preferably a Dutch oven, add olive oil and brown veal shanks on all sides. Transfer shanks to a plate when they are browned. Pour out any excess fat remaining in pan. Add wine and bring to a boil, deglazing the pan. Add stock and simmer 2 minutes. Place thyme, basil, and bay leaves to the pot. Add onion, celery, carrots, and garlic and continue cooking until vegetables are slightly softened, about 5 minutes. Add tomatoes and tomato juice and simmer another 5 minutes. Return shanks to pot, cover tightly, and bring to a simmer over moderately high heat. Place in hot oven for 2½ hours, checking periodically to make sure the liquid has not reduced too much. If so, add stock as needed.

While shanks are in the oven prepare gremolata. In a small bowl combine parsley, lemon rind, and garlic. Add gremolata just before serving.

Serves 4

You may have to order the veal shanks ahead of time, even from a specialty meat shop.

When you return shanks to the pot, be sure there is enough liquid to just cover the veal. Too much and the dish will come out like soup, too little and the meat dries out. If you need more liquid, add stock or more wine, not water. Mashed potatoes or a saffron-infused risotto are the most traditional side dishes serves with this entrée.

MAIN COURSES

Duck Breast with Green Peppercorn Sauce

1 tablespoon green peppercorns
6 duck breasts
½ teaspoon salt
½ teaspoon pepper
2 tablespoons flour
3 tablespoons butter or more
6 shallots, finely chopped
2 tablespoons cognac
½ cup chicken stock
Salt to taste
1½ cups heavy cream
Parsley
Cooked wild rice

Preheat oven to 180°F. Put peppercorns in 2 tablespoons of warm water to soften. Pull skin off breast area of the duck and cut the breast section off. Clean the breast; pat dry, and cut into thick "French fry" slices. Mix ½ teaspoon of salt and pepper together with flour. Dust each breast with flour mixture and fry in 3 tablespoons of butter in a Dutch oven for three minutes on each side for rare. Add more butter as needed for frying. The breast should look pink inside. Be careful not to overcook! Drain well and place in oven to keep warm.

Sauté shallots in pan drippings. Crush the peppercorns that have been soaking in water and add this mixture. Cook for 5 minutes, smashing the peppercorns with cooking spoon. Add cognac and ignite. Spoon gently until fire goes out. Add chicken stock and bring mixture to a boil. Lower heat, slowly add cream, and cook until mixture thickens. Sprinkle with parsley and taste for salt. Place duck breast on warm plates and pour sauce on top. Serve with freshly steamed wild rice.

Serves 4

If you've been reluctant to try rare duck, give this recipe a try; it just may win you over. A family favorite way to eat wild duck!

131

MAIN COURSES

Doc's Pheasant Madeira

6   pheasant breasts, cleaned and skinned

Flour

Paprika

Salt and pepper to taste

¾   cup butter

1   cup Madeira wine

1   pint half-and-half

1   10-ounce can whole artichoke hearts

Preheat oven to 350°F. Tenderize pheasant breasts if needed. Sprinkle with salt, pepper, and paprika. Dip in half-and-half and dust with flour. In a large ovenproof skillet, sauté breast in 2 tablespoons butter. When golden brown, add wine and bake for 1 hour. Remove from oven and add ½ cup or more of half-and-half to thicken gravy. Garnish with artichokes. Delicious served with warm wild rice.

Serves 6

Excellent way to eat wild game!

M
A
I
N

C
O
U
R
S
E
S

Red Snapper Vera Cruz

1   medium onion, chopped

3   cloves garlic, minced

¼   cup water

1   16-ounce can diced tomatoes, undrained

⅓   cup sliced pitted green or ripe olives

1   tablespoon lime juice

1-2   teaspoons of chopped jalapeño peppers

1   teaspoon sugar

1   pound skinless red snapper fillets or other white fish, ½-inch thick

Hot cooked rice

For the sauce, combine onion, garlic, and water in a saucepan. Bring to a boil, reduce heat and cover. Simmer for about 3-4 minutes until onions are tender. Stir in tomatoes, olives, lime juice, peppers, and sugar. Return to a boil, reduce heat, and cover for 7 minutes. Uncover and simmer another 15 minutes. Preheat oven to 450°F. While sauce is cooking, place fish fillets in a 12x8x2-inch glass ovenproof baking dish, tucking under any thin edges. Spoon sauce on top of fish and bake for 10-15 minutes, or until fish flakes easily when tested with a fork. Serve over rice.

Serves 2-3

You can add green bell pepper slices or other fresh vegetables with or without the jalapeño peppers, depending on how spicy you like it.

Catfish Charlie with Buttery Pecan Sauce

1	cup flour
4	teaspoons Cajun seasoning
2	eggs, beaten
½	cup milk
6	ounces catfish fillets
½	cup canola or peanut oil
1	stick butter
1	cup pecan pieces
4	tablespoons chopped parsley
2	tablespoons minced garlic
2	tablespoons lemon juice
¼	cup Worcestershire sauce
¼	cup heavy cream
1	teaspoon coarse salt
¼	teaspoon cayenne pepper

In a shallow bowl, combine flour with Cajun seasoning. Dredge fillets in flour, coating evenly. Dip fillets in egg mixture, dredge again in the flour, and place fillets on paper towel. Heat oil in heavy skillet. When hot, lay fillets in the skillet and fry for 3-4 minutes on each side until golden brown. Transfer to a warm platter.

Discard any oil remaining in skillet and wipe clean with a paper towel. Return skillet to stove and melt butter over medium-high heat. When butter foams, add pecan pieces and stir constantly for about 1½ minutes, until pecans are lightly toasted. Add parsley, garlic, lemon juice, Worcestershire sauce, and cream. Stir with a whisk for about 15 seconds and remove from heat. Add salt, cayenne pepper, and remaining 6 tablespoons of butter (cut into small pieces) and stir until butter melts completely. Pour sauce over fillets and serve immediately.

Serves 4

MAIN COURSES

Black pepper, garlic powder, salt and cayenne pepper are excellent "after cooking" seasonings. Allow guests to season dishes with these spices at the table.

Seared Yellow Fin Tuna

4   8-ounce tuna steaks
2   tablespoons fennel seeds, crushed
½   cup olive oil
¼   cup soy sauce
1   tablespoon sherry
2   tablespoons molasses or honey
2   cloves garlic, minced
1   tablespoon freshly squeezed lemon juice
½   teaspoon ginger
2   teaspoons ground cumin
¼   teaspoon cayenne pepper
    Freshly ground black pepper to taste

Combine fennel seeds, olive oil, soy sauce, sherry, molasses or honey, garlic, lemon juice, ginger, cumin, cayenne pepper, and black pepper in a bowl with a cover and mix well. Add tuna steaks, cover well, and refrigerate for at least 6 hours, turning frequently. Drain steaks and discard marinade. Grill steaks on medium-high heat for 3 minutes per side for medium-rare or to desired doneness. Serve tuna steaks with oven-roasted potatoes and grilled asparagus for a healthy and delectable meal!

Serves 4

134

M A I N C O U R S E S

Apple and Horseradish Glazed Salmon

⅓   cup apple jelly
2   tablespoons prepared horseradish
1   tablespoon apple cider vinegar
2   tablespoons apple butter
½   teaspoon kosher salt, divided
1   tablespoon finely chopped fresh chives
4   wild salmon fillets or pieces of wild salmon
¼   teaspoon freshly ground black pepper
2   teaspoons olive or sesame oil

Preheat oven to 350°F. Combine apple jelly, horseradish, vinegar, apple butter, and ¼ teaspoon salt in a microwave-safe bowl, stirring well with a whisk. Heat mixture on high for 1 minute, or until apple jelly melts. Slightly cool mixture and add chives, stirring well.

Sprinkle salmon with ¼ teaspoon salt and pepper. Heat oil in a large, ovenproof nonstick skillet over medium heat. Add salmon and cook 3 minutes. Turn salmon over and brush with half of apple mixture. Bake in oven for about 8-10 minutes, or until fish flakes easily when tested with a fork. Brush with remaining apple mixture and serve.

Serves 4

Salmon Fillets with Basil

2 lemons
4 6-ounce salmon fillets, cleaned
   and boned
4 tablespoons unsalted butter,
   cut into 6 pieces
2 tablespoons olive oil
1 tablespoon minced shallots
2 teaspoons minced garlic
1 cup stemmed and torn fresh
   basil leaves
   Pinch of cayenne pepper
   Salt and freshly ground black
   pepper to taste
1 cup heavy cream, room
   temperature
¼ cup coarsely chopped fresh
   basil for garnish

Preheat oven to 200°F. Squeeze 1 lemon over the salmon, making sure to coat both sides. Melt 2 tablespoons of butter and the oil over medium heat in a sauté pan large enough to accommodate the 4 fillets. When butter and oil start to foam, add the fillets. Cook for 3-5 minutes on each side. Transfer to an ovenproof plate, and place in oven.

Add remaining butter to the pan, one piece at a time, and melt until foaming. Add shallots and garlic and cook until soft about 2 minutes. Add juice from the other lemon, basil leaves, cayenne pepper, salt, and pepper and stir to combine well. Add the heavy cream very slowly to prevent curdling and bring to a simmer. Cook until sauce is reduced by a third. Adjust seasonings to taste.

Place the fish on warm plates or a platter with a small pool of sauce underneath each fillet. Top each fillet lightly with a little more sauce and sprinkle with the basil.

Serves 4

135

> Thaw frozen fish in milk for a
> fresh flavor and to eliminate the frozen taste.

Honey-Glazed Salmon with Apples

SALMON MARINADE
½ cup rice wine vinegar
2 shallots, chopped
2 tablespoons honey
1 tablespoon whole seed mustard
4 ½-pound salmon fillets or 1 (2½-pound) slab fillet, skinless
1 Granny Smith apple, thinly sliced
1 bag organic mixed greens

GLAZE
½ cup honey
2 tablespoons whole seed mustard

In a small saucepan heat vinegar, shallots, honey, and mustard seed. Let cool. Place salmon in a glass dish and pour marinade over it. Refrigerate at least for two hours in the refrigerator. Take fish out of marinade and place it in an ovenproof dish. Discard marinade.

To cook, preheat oven to 350°F. In a microwave-safe bowl, heat the honey and mustard for one minute. Drizzle hot mixture over salmon and place in oven for 18 minutes. Turn the oven to broil and brown the salmon about 3 minutes.

To serve, place greens on individual dinner plates with sliced apples on top. Place salmon on top of greens and pour warm juices over top of salmon. This dish goes well with rice pilaf and lemon sorbet with blueberries for dessert.

Serves 4

A very good friend of ours is an airline pilot who had many Paris layovers. Since he was in Paris so often, he decided to take cooking lessons at the "Cordon Bleu" cooking school. A few years ago he brought his wife and family to our home for a ski holiday and prepared this meal for us. We are so impressed with our friend's cooking, I had to include one of his many positively spectacular recipes.

136

Basted Grilled Wild Salmon

½ cup firmly packed brown sugar
½ cup dry white wine
¼ cup lemon juice
½ teaspoon salt
¼ teaspoon pepper
8 6-ounce wild salmon fillets, boned, skinned, and maximum 1¼-inch thick
¼ cup butter
Lemon wedges for garnish

In large wide bowl or 9x13-inch baking dish, stir brown sugar, wine, lemon juice, salt, and pepper until sugar is dissolved. Rinse fish and pat dry. Add to marinade and turn to coat. Cover and chill for 1-2 hours. Lift salmon from marinade and transfer to a 12x17-inch ovenproof baking pan. Pour marinade into a 1½-2-quart pan over medium-high heat. Add butter and stir until butter is melted and mixture is simmering for 4-5 minutes.

Lay salmon on generously oiled grill over solid bed of medium-hot coals or medium-high heat on gas grill. Baste fish generously and close lid if using gas grill. Cook until salmon pieces are well browned on bottom 3½-4 minutes. With a wide spatula, carefully turn pieces. Brush tops with sauce and continue to cook about 5-6 minutes longer, basting often, until salmon is just opaque but still moist-looking in center of thickest part (cut to test). Discard any remaining sauce. Transfer salmon to warm platter and garnish with lemon wedges. Add more salt and pepper if needed.

Serves 8

This recipe is from a lodge in Juneau, Alaska, where the grilled salmon is legendary.

137

M
A
I
N

C
O
U
R
S
E
S

Mediterranean Skillet — A Calamari Delight

3 pounds squid
2 large onions, chopped
½ dried chili pepper
3 red potatoes per person, quartered
1 ounce olive oil
1 tablespoon tomato paste or two fresh peeled tomatoes
Salt to taste
Pepper to taste
Rice or noodles

Rinse squid. Remove plastic-like lining from inside and cut squid into bite-size pieces. In a large skillet, sauté onions in olive oil for a few minutes on medium heat. Add the squid and cook slowly for approximately 5 minutes. Add potatoes, chili pepper, and 2 cups water along with tomato paste. Continue cooking for approximately 1 hour, adding salt and pepper to taste. Add additional water if necessary. Serve with rice or noodles.

Serves 4-6

This dish actually came from a woman who was a citizen of Malta. She made a lot of new and interesting dishes to treat our taste buds while living up Golden Gate Canyon. The elevation was equivalent to many of ours at 9,500 feet, and she adapted quite well to the changes necessary in cooking between sea level and high altitude.

Curried Shrimp

1½ pounds shrimp, peeled and deveined
1 teaspoon dark rum
Dash of salt
1 teaspoon sugar
⅓ cup mild curry powder
3 tablespoons olive oil
Cilantro sprigs
2 limes, cut in wedges

Sprinkle shrimp with rum. Let stand about 20 minutes and pat dry. Sprinkle evenly with salt and sugar. Dust shrimp with curry powder. Heat 1 tablespoon of oil in large skillet over medium heat. Add enough shrimp to cover the bottom of pan in a single layer. Cook until shrimp are brown and crisp about 2 minutes per side. Keep warm while cooking remaining shrimp. Arrange shrimp on cilantro and garnish with lime wedges.

Serves 8-10

Scallops in Sherry Cream Sauce

2	tablespoons butter
1	pound bay scallops, rinsed and patted dry
2	tablespoons minced shallots
½	cup sliced mushrooms
⅓	cup dry sherry
2	egg yolks
½	cup heavy cream
	Salt and pepper to taste

Heat 1 tablespoon of butter in a large skillet over medium-high heat until the foam subsides. Add scallops and sauté, stirring occasionally, for 3-4 minutes or until opaque and slightly firm. Remove from skillet and keep warm. Heat the remaining tablespoon of butter in skillet until foam subsides. Add shallots and mushrooms and sauté for 2 minutes, stirring occasionally. Add sherry and bring to a boil. Lower heat and simmer for 3 minutes. In a small bowl, whisk together egg yolks and cream. Gradually whisk egg mixture into the mushroom mixture and add salt and pepper. Return scallops to the skillet and coat well with the sauce. Serve immediately.

Serves 2

Baked Shrimp Scampi

2	pounds raw shrimp, peeled and deveined
2	tablespoons lemon juice
½	cup olive oil
3	tablespoons dried parsley
3	tablespoons fresh parsley
1	teaspoon dry mustard
½	teaspoon salt
½	teaspoon pepper
4	cloves garlic, chopped
	French bread

Preheat oven to 500°F. Combine lemon juice, olive oil, dried and fresh parsley, mustard, salt, pepper, and garlic. Pour over shrimp and marinate about 30 minutes. Place shrimp with marinade in a 9x13-inch casserole dish 4 inches away from heat. Cook 5 minutes, turn shrimp, and cook 5 more minutes, or until shrimp are opaque in the center. Serve with French bread for sopping the sauce.

Serves 4-6

This recipe came from friends (actually, the parents of my college softball teammate) after we just happened to run into them in Tucson, Arizona. We had stayed one night in a cheap motel, and they offered to let us stay in their brand new house — then proceeded to feed us!

139

Lieux Lobster Thermidor

6	1-pound lobsters, either fresh or frozen
	Water, enough to cover lobster
2	cloves garlic, chopped
1	onion, chopped
1	celery stalk, cut into pieces
½	cup salt
2	teaspoons black pepper
½	pound fresh mushrooms, sliced
1	tablespoon butter

SAUCE

5	tablespoons butter
6	tablespoons flour
1½-2	cups lobster broth
½	cup whipping cream
2	egg yolks
	Dash dry mustard
⅛	teaspoon cayenne pepper
	Pepper to taste
½	cup dry sherry
4	dashes paprika
3	tablespoons chopped parsley
3-4	tablespoons whipping cream
	Parmesan cheese

In a large pot, boil lobster tails in water that has been seasoned with garlic, onion, celery, salt, and pepper. Boil for 30 minutes. Let stand in water for an additional 10 minutes and cool. Remove from pot and remove meat from the tails. Dice into ⅜-inch cubes. Set meat aside and reserve shells. Boil lobster broth down rapidly until liquid has reduced to approximately 2 cups. Reserve liquid.

In a small skillet, sauté lobster meat and mushrooms in 1 tablespoon of butter for 5 minutes. Pour off excess liquid and set aside.

Preheat oven to 450°F. In a medium saucepan, cook 5 tablespoons butter and flour slowly together without browning, stirring constantly. Remove from heat and beat in 1½ cups lobster broth. Return to heat and boil for 1 minute and set aside.

In another bowl, blend cream, egg yolks, mustard, and cayenne pepper, and pepper to taste. Slowly stir the lobster broth into this mixture. Return the sauce to the pan and bring to a boil for 2 minutes, stirring constantly. Add sherry, paprika, and fresh parsley, stirring gently for 5 minutes. Thin sauce, if needed, with remaining 3-4 tablespoons cream.

Arrange the lobster shells on a baking tray. Fill shells with the mixture, sprinkle generously with Parmesan cheese, and bake for 15 minutes. Lobster Thermidor makes a beautiful presentation placed on a plate with a scoop of rice pilaf in the curve of the shell, surrounded by steamed vegetables.

Serves 6

140

MAIN COURSES

Shrimp à la Rockefeller

1½ pounds fresh or frozen shrimp, peeled, deveined, cooked, and drained
¼ cup chopped onion
¼ cup butter
¼ cup flour
½ teaspoon dry mustard
1 teaspoon salt
2 cups milk
½ cup shredded Swiss cheese
¼ cup grated Parmesan cheese, divided
2 packages frozen chopped spinach, cooked and drained
2 tablespoons lemon juice
1 cup water chestnuts, drained and sliced

Preheat oven to 400°F. In a skillet over medium heat, sauté onion in butter until tender, not brown. Stir in flour, salt, and mustard. Add milk, stirring constantly, until thickened. Remove from heat. Add Swiss cheese, stir until melted, and fold in ½ of the Parmesan cheese.

Mix spinach and water chestnuts. Arrange vegetables in a shallow 2-quart baking dish and drizzle lemon juice over vegetables. Arrange shrimp on vegetables. Pour sauce over shrimp, sprinkle with remaining Parmesan cheese, and bake in oven for 15-20 minutes or until hot and bubbly.

Serves 6 (for 12, double recipe plus another half of sauce)

Serve over rice.

Spicy Shrimp with Rice

¼ cup white wine
3 tablespoons soy sauce
2 tablespoons sugar
1 tablespoon vegetable oil
2 teaspoons dried parsley flakes
⅛-¼ teaspoon ground ginger
Dash of hot pepper sauce
1 pound jumbo raw shrimp, peeled, shelled and deveined
Cooked rice

Mix all ingredients except shrimp in medium bowl. Stir in shrimp, cover, and marinate at room temperature for 45 minutes or 3 hours in refrigerator.

Preheat oven for broiling. Remove shrimp from marinade, reserving marinade. Place shrimp in round ovenproof baking pan. Broil 6-8 minutes, brushing with marinade halfway through cooking.

Serves 4

Shrimp and Andouille Sausage

½ cup hot pepper sauce
⅓ cup dry white wine
1 large shallot, chopped
1 tablespoon lemon juice
1 tablespoon white wine vinegar
½ cup heavy cream
¼ cup olive oil
½ pound smoked andouille sausage, sliced
1 red bell pepper, diced
1 green bell pepper, diced
1 medium onion, finely chopped
5 cloves garlic, finely minced
½ cup dry white wine
1 14.5-ounce can diced tomatoes in juice
4 Roma tomatoes, deseeded and diced
1 teaspoon red pepper flakes, or to taste
¼ cup fresh parsley, chopped
2 pounds raw medium shrimp, (21-25 count), peeled and deveined

Combine hot pepper sauce, wine, shallots, lemon juice, and vinegar in a heavy saucepan. Boil about 15 minutes over medium-high heat until reduced to ½ cup. Stir in heavy cream. This can be made ahead, cooled, and re-warmed just before serving.

Heat olive oil in a Dutch oven over medium heat. Add sausage and brown stirring occasionally. Remove sausage and set aside. Add peppers, onions, and garlic and sauté for 10 minutes, or until vegetables are tender. Return sausage to the Dutch oven and add white wine; cook to reduce wine by half. Add tomatoes, red pepper flakes, and parsley and bring to a boil. Add shrimp stirring constantly just until shrimp are cooked through (do not over-cook shrimp.)

Spoon shrimp and sausage over Lip Smackin' Grits and top with the hot pepper cream sauce.

Serves 6

M A I N   C O U R S E S

Barley Mushroom Burgers

½ cup uncooked Quick Cooking Barley
1 large egg, well beaten
1 cup ricotta cheese
1 cup Cheddar cheese, shredded
1 cup mushrooms, minced
½ cup dried breadcrumbs
¼ cup fresh parsley, minced
Salt and pepper to taste
Cooking spray

Cook barley according to package directions. Combine egg, ricotta cheese, Cheddar cheese, mushrooms, breadcrumbs, parsley, salt, and pepper. Stir barley into egg mixture. Form patties. Spray a large non-stick pan or griddle with cooking spray. When pan is hot, place patties in pan, not overcrowding pan. Cook until mixture is firm and cheese has melted, turning as needed.

Serves 4

Quick and easy, this is a vegetarian delight.

Mizutaki

SAUCE

9	ounces toasted white sesame seeds
¾	cup soy sauce
¾	cup sesame or vegetable oil
3	tablespoons vinegar
⅓	cup water
3	cloves garlic, crushed

BEEF AND VEGETABLES

2	cups cooked rice
1	package tofu, cut into ½-inch chunks
1-2	cans bamboo shoots
1	pound thinly sliced beef (tenderloin works well)
½	pound large mushrooms, thinly sliced
2	bunches spinach leaves, stemmed
1	bunch scallions, cut into 1½-inch length

Sauce: Grind sesame seeds in blender at high speed. Mix well with remaining ingredients, using more or less water as desired. Divide into 4 small sauce bowls and set aside.

Heat hot water in electric frying pan or wok to simmer. Add tofu until warm and then add bamboo shoots. Add beef, mushrooms, spinach, and scallions. Cook to desired doneness, about 5 minutes. When meat and vegetables are cooked, remove with slotted spoon, careful not to mix in water from cooking pot, and put in sauce bowls. Pour meat/vegetable/ sauce mixture over hot rice.

After main meal, spoon some of the cooking liquid into what remains in the sauce bowls and drink as a soup.

Serves 4

143

Feta Pie

	Olive oil
1	medium onion, chopped
2	bunches fresh spinach, stemmed, rinsed and chopped
1	16-ounce feta cheese, crumbled
2	eggs, lightly beaten
1	cup fresh dill, chopped
2	tablespoons fresh parsley, minced
	Pepper to taste
6	phyllo dough sheets
4	tablespoons butter, melted

Preheat oven to 350°F. In a medium-sized skillet, over medium heat, sauté onions in oil until transparent. Add spinach. Mix feta, eggs, dill, parsley, and pepper. In a buttered 8x12-inch ovenproof baking dish, place 3 sheets of phyllo dough spreading each with the melted butter. Spread spinach on top, add the feta mix, and top with 3 more phyllo sheets spread with butter. Bake for 30-45 minutes.

Serves 4-6

Nice simple "light" dish – great with a Greek style salad or wedges of tomatoes with olive oil, basil, and pepper.

Layered Zucchini with Feta

¾ cup bulgur
¾ cup boiling water
2½ tablespoons vegetable oil
2 cups sliced onions
4 cloves garlic, minced or pressed
6 cups thinly sliced zucchini rounds
½ teaspoon dried oregano
½ teaspoon dried basil
½ teaspoon dried marjoram
⅛ teaspoon black pepper
2 eggs
1 cup grated feta cheese (5 ounces)
1 cup cottage cheese
1 cup chopped fresh parsley
2 tablespoons tomato paste
1 tablespoon soy sauce
1 cup grated Cheddar cheese (3 ounces)
2 medium tomatoes, thinly sliced
1½ tablespoons sesame seeds (optional)

Preheat oven to 350°F. Place bulgur in a bowl and pour in boiling water. Cover and set aside until bulgur has absorbed water and becomes soft and chewable.

Sauté onions and garlic in oil until onions are just translucent. Add zucchini, dried herbs, and black pepper. Continue to sauté on medium to low heat until the zucchini is tender, but not falling apart.

In a bowl, lightly beat eggs. Mix in feta and cottage cheese. Add chopped parsley, tomato paste, and soy sauce to the bulgur and mix well.

Assemble casserole in an oiled 9x9-inch casserole dish. Layer the bulgur mixture, the sautéed vegetables, and then the feta mixture. Top the casserole with grated Cheddar cheese, tomato slices, and a light sprinkling of sesame seeds. Cover and bake for 45 minutes. For crustier cheese, uncover casserole for the final 15 minutes of baking. Allow to sit for 5-10 minutes before serving.

Serves 4-6

144

MAIN COURSES

Italian Herb Seasoning
1 teaspoon dried oregano
1 teaspoon dried marjoram
1 teaspoon dried thyme
1 teaspoon dried basil
1 teaspoon dried rosemary
1 teaspoon dried sage

Chilaquiles

Butter or cooking spray
8   flour tortillas
1   8-ounce can diced green chilies
2-3 cups Pepper Jack cheese, grated
4   eggs
2   cups buttermilk
Salt and pepper to taste
Dash of basil, cumin, or oregano, if desired

OPTIONAL ADDITIONS

1   16-ounce can pinto or black beans
Sliced tofu or cooked chicken, chopped into pieces
1   cup chopped onion, lightly sautéed
1   small zucchini and/or squash, sliced or cubed and lightly sautéed
1-2 cloves garlic, minced and lightly browned

Preheat oven to 375°F. Butter a 2-quart casserole pan or a 9x13-inch ovenproof baking pan. Tear 2-3 tortillas into bite-size pieces and layer the bottom of the pan. Distribute half the chilies, half the cheese, and half of optional ingredients you are using over the tortillas. Repeat these steps. Make a final layer of tortillas on top.

Beat the eggs and buttermilk together with spices. Pour over the top of the casserole and gently use a knife or fork to poke around the edges to allow the mixture to seep down into the layers. Bake uncovered for 35 minutes.

Serves 4-6

This is an easy and filling dish that is great for brunch or a light dinner, served with a salad on the side.

145

Jerk Sauce

2	tablespoons ground allspice
2	tablespoons dried thyme
1½	teaspoons cayenne pepper
1½	teaspoons ground black pepper
3	teaspoons sage
1½	teaspoons ground cinnamon
2	tablespoons salt
4	tablespoons garlic powder
1	tablespoon sugar
¼	cup olive oil
¼	cup soy sauce
¾	cup white vinegar
½	cup orange juice
	Juice of two limes
1	Scotch Bonnet pepper (jalapeño or Serrano pepper is fine) finely ground
1	cup chopped onion
3	green onions, chopped

In a large bowl, combine allspice, thyme, cayenne pepper, black pepper, sage, cinnamon, salt, garlic powder, and sugar. Slowly whisk in olive oil, soy sauce, white vinegar, orange juice, and lime juice. Add onions and peppers and mix. Marinate for at least one hour. Use on grilled or sautéed meats.

We use this marinade for chicken breasts and fish (scallops, shrimp). It doesn't work so well on a whole roasted chicken.

Makes enough to marinate up to 5 pounds meat or fish.

To substitute honey for sugar, start by substituting up to half of the sugar. With a little experimentation, honey can replace all the sugar in some recipes.

SIDE
DISHES

Contents

Grilled Artichokes

2-3 whole fresh artichokes
Juice of 1 lemon
Sea salt
Olive oil

Wash and trim artichokes of thorns, leave 1 inch of stem. Cut each artichoke in half through the stem and carefully remove fuzz, being careful not to cut too much of the fleshy heart. Put artichoke halves back together and place in artichoke steamer or wedge into a pot with 1-2 inches of water. Drizzle with olive oil and ½ of the lemon juice. Sprinkle liberally with sea salt. Steam artichokes until tender, about 45-60 minutes. Place steamed artichoke halves on a platter, cut sides up, and drizzle again with olive oil, remaining lemon juice and more sea salt.

Place leaf side down on a medium heat grill. Turn frequently until outer leaves begin to curl and char.

Serves 4-6

Makes a great appetizer or side dish for a summer meal.

Asparagus with Hazelnut Sauce

2 pounds fresh asparagus spears
½ cup butter
4 ounces finely chopped hazelnuts
Pinch of tarragon
2 teaspoons wine vinegar
Salt to taste

Wash asparagus spears and break off bottom inch or so of each spear. Steam asparagus in steamer over boiling salted water until tender, about 12-15 minutes. Remove from heat and drain water. Arrange on serving dish and keep warm. Melt butter in saucepan until warm, but not browned, add tarragon and nuts, cook 1 minute. Add wine vinegar, stir once. Pour sauce over asparagus and serve immediately.

Serves 6

Puerto Rican Black Beans

¼ onion, diced
¼ green bell pepper, diced
1 clove garlic, minced
1 tablespoon olive oil
1 15-ounce can black beans
⅔ teaspoon salt
⅓ teaspoon red pepper
1 chicken bouillon cube
⅛ teaspoon ground cumin
½ teaspoon chopped fresh cilantro
¼ teaspoon dried oregano
1 bay leaf
½ teaspoon sugar
½ teaspoon vinegar

In a large saucepan, simmer onion, green pepper and garlic in oil about 15 minutes. Add beans, salt, red pepper, bouillon, cumin, cilantro, oregano, bay leaf, sugar and vinegar. Simmer 30 minutes, stirring occasionally.

To serve as soup, add 1¼ cups water to the basic recipe. Simmer about an hour. Flavor will be enhanced if the soup is refrigerated overnight. Heat and serve over cooked rice.

Serves 6

To serve as an entrée, add 2 tablespoons tomato sauce, diced green olives, a small diced cooked potato, and diced ham or chicken to the basic recipe. Serve with saffron rice.

---

1 cup of uncooked, long grain white rice makes 3 cups cooked rice. For fluffier, whiter rice, add 1 teaspoon of lemon juice per quart of water. To add extra flavor and nutrition to rice, cook in liquid reserved from cooking vegetables.

Red Cabbage and Apples

2 white or yellow onions, chopped
2 tablespoons cooking oil
1 head red cabbage, cut in pieces
½ cup vinegar
¾ cup water
1 teaspoon caraway seed
1 tablespoon brown sugar
1 apple, thinly sliced

In a large pot, sauté onions in oil until translucent. Add remaining ingredients and cook over medium low heat for 20 minutes, until cabbage is tender.

Serves 6

Caponata
Eggplant Antipasto

1	eggplant, peeled
4	stalks celery
⅓	cup olive oil
	Freshly ground black pepper
1	cup chopped onions
1	14-ounce can diced tomatoes
3	tablespoons wine vinegar
½	cup sugar
2	tablespoons drained capers
12	small green stuffed olives
1	tablespoon pine nuts

Cut eggplant into ½-inch pieces, put into a colander, sprinkle with salt and let drain for 30 minutes, pat eggplant dry with paper towel. Cut celery to fit a medium saucepan, add cold water just to cover. Bring to boil and simmer for 5 minutes, drain and cut celery into ¼-inch pieces. Heat 3 tablespoons oil in a frying pan and fry eggplant, stirring and turning frequently, about 10 minutes, until golden. Remove from pan, drain, and season with salt and pepper. Heat remaining oil in a second pan and sauté onion gently for 5 minutes. Add chopped celery, and sauté 5 minutes, then add tomatoes. Salt and pepper to taste. Gently simmer 10 minutes or until celery is tender; add vinegar, sugar, capers, olives, pine nuts and eggplant. Stir and simmer a few minutes more. Taste and adjust the seasoning, if desired. Cool, then store in the refrigerator.

Arrange on serving dish and serve cold, alone or surrounded with tuna or quartered hard-boiled eggs.

Serves 4-6

Makes a great appetizer or side dish for eggplant lovers!

Carrots with Maple-Balsamic Browned Butter

3¼ cups sliced peeled carrots, ¼-inch thick
1 tablespoon butter
1 tablespoon real maple syrup
1 teaspoon balsamic vinegar
⅛ teaspoon salt
⅛ teaspoon freshly ground pepper
1 teaspoon chopped fresh parsley

Steam carrot slices, covered, 15 minutes or until tender. Drain and set aside. Melt butter in a medium non-stick skillet over medium heat. Cook butter 3 minutes or until lightly browned, stirring constantly to prevent burning. Add syrup, vinegar, salt and pepper, stir until combined. Add carrots, cook 1 minute or until thoroughly heated, stirring to coat. Stir in parsley.

Serves 4

Double the maple-balsamic butter mixture for more sauce!

Carrot and Potato Gratin

2 pounds baking potatoes, peeled, thinly sliced
1½ pounds large carrots, peeled, thinly sliced
½ teaspoon salt
 Pepper
6 ounces grated Gruyére cheese
1 cup chicken stock or canned broth
4 tablespoons unsalted butter

Position rack in top third of oven and preheat to 375°F. Bring large pot of salted water to a boil. Add sliced baking potatoes and sliced carrots, cover and cook 5 minutes. Drain well. In a large, buttered glass baking dish, arrange ¼ of cooked vegetables. Sprinkle with ⅛ teaspoon salt and generous amount of pepper. Sprinkle with ¼ of grated cheese over the top. Repeat, layering 3 more times. Pour chicken stock over vegetables. Dot with butter. Cover and bake until chicken stock is absorbed and vegetables are tender, about 1 hour. Remove and bake uncovered about 10 minutes, until top is golden brown. Let stand 10 minutes before serving.

Serves 8

Cauliflower Cheddar Gratin with Horseradish Crumbs

3 pounds cauliflower, cut into ½-inch florets
¼ cup butter
2 tablespoons flour
1½ cups whole milk
2 cups coarsely grated sharp Cheddar cheese
½ cup finely chopped scallions
½ teaspoon salt
½ teaspoon black pepper
20 saltine crackers
2 tablespoons bottled horseradish, drained

Preheat oven to 350°F. In a large stockpot, cook cauliflower in boiling water until just tender, 6-8 minutes. Drain well and transfer to a buttered 2-quart baking dish. Melt 2 tablespoons butter over low heat and whisk in flour to make a roux. Slowly add milk to a boil, whisking frequently, until sauce thickens. Remove from heat and add cheese, scallions, salt and pepper. Whisk until cheese is melted. Pour sauce over cauliflower and stir to combine. In a bowl, coarsely crumble crackers. Melt remaining butter in a small saucepan, remove from heat and stir in horseradish. Pour over crumbs, toss to coat and sprinkle over cauliflower. Bake 15 minutes or until hot and bubbly. Can be made ahead and then warmed in a microwave oven.

Serves 8

Fresh Corn Pudding

2 cups fresh or frozen corn kernels
3 eggs, beaten
1 teaspoon sugar
2 teaspoons flour
½ teaspoon salt
½ teaspoon pepper
2 cups milk
2 teaspoons butter, broken up

Preheat oven to 350°F. Cut fresh corn from cob, scrape for additional corn milk. Beat eggs, add sugar, flour, salt and pepper, mix together, Pour over corn, stir, add milk, stir again. Top with butter chunks. Mixture will look milky and thin but cooks to custard consistency. Bake 45 minutes, or 1 hour if recipe is doubled.

Serves 6

Tomato Cauliflower Gratinée

3 tablespoons butter
1 cup chopped onion
3 large tomatoes, peeled and
   chopped
1 teaspoon sweet basil
   Salt and freshly ground black
   pepper to taste
1 head cauliflower
1 teaspoon salt
1 cup grated Swiss cheese
½ cup bread crumbs
   Fresh chopped parsley

Break cauliflower into florettes. Cook in boiling salted water for 10 minutes, until just tender. Drain cauliflower, refresh with cold water, toss with 1 teaspoon salt and drain again in a colander about 30 minutes.

Preheat over to 350°F. Melt butter and sauté onion. Add tomatoes, basil, salt and pepper. Cook 5 minutes on high heat to reduce excess juice. Stir cauliflower into tomato mixture. Pour all into a buttered baking dish. Mix bread crumbs with parsley and grated cheese. Sprinkle bread crumb and cheese mixture over tomato and cauliflower mixture. Bake for 20-30 minutes.

Serves 4-6

A 28-ounce can of diced tomatoes, drained, may be substituted for fresh tomatoes.

S
I
D
E

D
I
S
H
E
S

Cranberry-Apple Stuffing

¼ cup butter
¼ cup chopped onion
1 cup chopped celery
2½ cups chopped peeled apples
¼ cup packed brown sugar
1 16-ounce can whole-cranberry
   sauce
½ cup orange juice
½ cup raisins
1 7-ounce package herb-
   seasoned croutons

In large saucepan, melt butter over low heat. Add onion, celery and apples. Cook, stirring frequently, until almost tender. Remove from heat. Add sugar, cranberry sauce, orange juice, raisins, stir until mixed. Add croutons all at once, tossing lightly until evenly moistened. Makes about 7 cups.

Serves 4-6

This stuffing is a family favorite every Thanksgiving.

Cook stuffing in a separate casserole dish while roasting the turkey.

Maque Choux

12 ears tender fresh corn
4 tablespoons butter or bacon drippings
1 onion, chopped fine
1 green bell pepper, chopped small
1 clove garlic, minced
  Salt and fresh ground black pepper to taste
  Dash hot pepper sauce
1 cup milk or cream

Using a large cutting board, cut corn off cob and scrape to get all the corn milk, place in large bowl and set aside. Heat margarine or bacon drippings in heavy cast iron Dutch oven, add onion, bell pepper, and garlic. Sauté until tender.

Add corn, salt, pepper, garlic and hot pepper sauce. Cook mixture over medium heat for 1 hour, stirring often. Mixture should brown on bottom of pot, but not stick; scrape bottom of pot to get "crusty" part mixed in with rest of corn. Add milk as needed, a little at a time, to keep mixture moist. Corn will be tender and have a golden brown luster when done.

Variation: add shrimp or chicken pieces, which have been grilled in a little butter or olive oil to the corn in the last 15 minutes.

Serves 12 as a side dish.

This recipe is from south Louisiana and is a wonderful dish to make with fresh sweet corn in season. The name is thought to come from a French interpretation of the Native American name for this dish.

SIDE DISHES

Roasted Spicy Corn

4 ears fresh sweet corn, in husks
1 teaspoon Hungarian paprika
½ teaspoon onion powder
½ teaspoon kosher salt
¼ teaspoon dried thyme
¼ teaspoon dried oregano
⅛ teaspoon cayenne
4 tablespoons unsalted butter, softened

Submerge the ears of corn in cold water and soak for at least 30 minutes. Drain. In a small bowl, mix together paprika, onion powder, salt, thyme, oregano and cayenne. Add butter and mash with the back of a fork, then stir. Pull back husks on each ear of corn, leaving them attached at the stem. Remove corn silk. Spread 1 tablespoon of seasoned butter evenly over the kernels of each ear. Fold husks back over the kernels. Use string or a thin strip of husk to tie the top. Grill corn until tender, 25-30 minutes, turning 3 or 4 times. Husks may become brown or burn. Remove from grill. When cool enough to handle, carefully pull husks back and cut off. Serve immediately.

Serves 4

Ojai Green Beans

12 ounces sugar snap peas, green beans or wax beans

DRESSING
1½ teaspoons chopped shallots
½ teaspoon Dijon mustard
3 teaspoons champagne vinegar
½ teaspoon ground black pepper
1½ tablespoons olive oil
½ cup pomegranate seeds
2 tablespoons toasted walnuts

Wash beans, blanch in boiling salted water, 2-4 minutes, then drain. Stir together dressing ingredients. Add dressing to beans and toss. Garnish with pomegranate seeds. Top each serving with toasted walnuts. Serve warm or cold.

Serves 4

This recipe is from Ojai, a beautiful spot in Southern California.

Toasted nuts: place nuts in a pan, in a single even layer. Brown nuts over low heat for 10-15 minutes, stirring occasionally, until nuts are brown and fragrant. Watch carefully, nuts burn easily.

Eggplant in the Style of Modugno

EGGPLANT

2	large eggplants, sliced lengthwise ¼-inch thick
1½	tablespoons salt
2	cups olive oil
½	cup bread crumbs
2-3	teaspoons minced garlic
½-¾	cup chopped parsley
3	cups grated mozzarella cheese
1½	cup grated Fontina cheese
½	cup grated Parmesan cheese
½	cup toasted pine nuts
1	large egg, beaten
	Salt to taste
	Freshly ground black pepper
	Fresh chopped basil

MARINARA SAUCE

¼	cup olive oil
2	garlic cloves, crushed
2	28-ounce cans crushed tomatoes
¼	teaspoon salt
½	teaspoon freshly ground pepper

Layer eggplant slices in a colander, sprinkle each layer with salt. Set aside to drain for at least 1½ hours. Gently squeeze out the excess liquid. Pat dry with paper towels. In a large skillet, heat olive oil over moderately high heat about 1 minute. Add eggplant slices in small batches and fry, turning once, until golden and cooked through, about 2 minutes per side. Remove and drain on paper towels.

Preheat oven to 375°F. In a medium bowl, combine breadcrumbs, garlic, parsley, cheeses, and pine nuts. Stir in egg and season with salt and pepper to taste.

Marinara sauce: In a medium non-reactive skillet, heat oil over moderately low heat. Add garlic and cook, stirring until golden, about 4 minutes. Add tomatoes, salt and pepper. Cook about 30 minutes, until thickened, stirring occasionally. Soft bits of tomato will remain.

Spoon part of the marinara sauce into a non-reactive baking pan. Spread about 2 tablespoons of the mozzarella mixture on each slice of eggplant, roll up and place seam-side down in the pan. Spoon remaining marinara sauce over eggplant rolls, sprinkle with Parmesan and basil. This dish can be prepared to this point several hours ahead and kept covered at room temperature. Bake until mixture bubbles and cheese is melted, about 20 minutes. Serve at room temperature for fullest flavor, or serve hot.

Serves 8

These rolls make a wonderful antipasto or a delicious luncheon dish.

Indian Spiced Green Beans

⅓   cup water
5   garlic cloves, crushed
1   tablespoon fresh lemon juice
1   teaspoon salt
    Cayenne pepper to taste
     (start with ¼ teaspoon)
⅓   cup cooking oil
½   teaspoon cumin seeds
2   pounds fresh green beans,
     trimmed and cut into ¼-inch
     pieces

In a small bowl combine water, garlic, lemon juice, salt and cayenne pepper. In a large skillet, heat oil over medium high heat. Add cumin seeds and stir for 3-4 seconds. Add green beans and sauté for 1 minute. Stir in garlic liquid mixture, reduce heat to low, cook covered, stirring occasionally, for 20 minutes, or until the beans are tender. Increase heat to high and cook uncovered, stirring constantly, until liquid has all evaporated. Serve immediately.

Serves 6

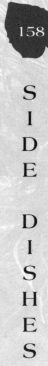

158

Garlic Cheese Grits

1   cup uncooked old fashioned
     grits (not quick or instant)
½   pound sharp or medium
     Cheddar, grated
1   stick butter
2   eggs, well beaten
1   garlic clove, pressed (or garlic
     powder to taste)
¼   cup milk
    Salt and pepper to taste
1   teaspoon Worcestershire sauce
    Hot pepper sauce

Cook grits according to directions on box, over low heat, stirring, until creamy and the consistency of thick sauce, but not congealed. Remove cooked grits to mixing bowl, stir in grated cheese, butter, eggs, salt and pepper, Worcestershire sauce, milk and hot pepper sauce. Put in a greased 1½-quart glass casserole. Bake 40 minutes to 1 hour at 300° to 350°F. Casserole is done when slightly browned. Don't overcook.

Serves 6-8

Refrigerate leftovers, then slice and broil in a little oil or butter the next morning to go with breakfast.

Grandma Dot's Green Beans

8   strips thick sliced bacon
1   tablespoon flour
1   medium onion
¼-½ cup white vinegar
¼-½ cup sugar
2   28-ounce cans green beans, drain and reserve juice or 3½ pounds fresh green beans
    Salt and pepper to taste

Cook bacon, crumble and set aside. Reserve enough bacon drippings to cover the bottom of the pan. Add flour and mix well. Sauté onion in drippings on medium until soft. Add ¼ cup vinegar and ¼ cup sugar to onion mixture. Add ¼ cup of reserved bean juice and simmer for 5 minutes. (To increase the sweet/tangy flavor, always add equal amounts of vinegar and sugar at the same time.) Stir in green beans and cook on medium until hot. Add bacon crumbles and simmer on low heat for 20-30 minutes to allow beans to absorb flavor. Beans can also be placed in a crock pot at this point and cooked on low for 8-10 hours. Add more of the reserved bean juice as needed to keep from getting too dry.

Serves 8-12

A favorite at every holiday dinner and family gathering.

This dish can be made with fresh green beans. Prepare according to directions, but substitute about 3 ½ pounds fresh green beans that have been trimmed and blanched. Simmer or cook in crock pot on low to desired tenderness. The dish can easily be doubled for a crowd by adjusting the amount of all ingredients to taste. Vinegar and sugar must ALWAYS be added in equal amounts, regardless of how much is added.

Lip "Smackin" Grits!

4   cups low salt chicken broth
1   cup heavy cream
6   tablespoons butter
3   garlic cloves, smashed and minced
1   cup uncooked coarse ground corn grits (also known as polenta)

Combine chicken broth, cream, butter and garlic in a heavy 2-quart saucepan and bring to a boil over high heat. Gradually whisk in grits, bring back to a boil, whisking constantly. Reduce heat to low and simmer, whisking often, until thickened, about 18 minutes.

Serves 6-8

Gourmet Macaroni and Cheese

4	strips cooked bacon, crumbled
1	large red onion, halved and sliced
6	ounces elbow macaroni
¼	cup of butter
3	tablespoons flour
1 ½	cups half-and-half, or light cream
¼-½	cup crumbled blue cheese
2	cups shredded mozzarella cheese
	Salt to taste
⅛	teaspoon pepper

Preheat oven to 350°F. In large skillet, cook bacon over medium heat until crisp, turning once, drain bacon and crumble. Reserve bacon drippings in skillet. Sauté onion in bacon drippings for 5-8 minutes until translucent. Set aside. Cook macaroni according to package directions. To prepare sauce, melt butter in saucepan over medium low heat, stirring. Slowly add flour, stirring constantly, until thoroughly mixed, and mixture starts to thicken. Slowly add half-and-half or cream, stirring constantly. Gradually add blue cheese and 1½ cups mozzarella, stir until cheese is melted. Remove from heat. Place macaroni in 1½-quart glass baking dish. Add bacon, onions, cheese sauce, and pepper. Toss gently to combine. Add salt and pepper to taste.

Bake uncovered for 20 minutes. Stir gently. Top with remaining mozzarella cheese. Bake 10 minutes more or until top of casserole is brown and bubbly. Let stand 10 minutes before serving.

Serves 6

Makes a beautiful casserole. There won't be any leftovers!

Reserve a small amount of crumbled bacon and onion slices for garnish. Sprinkle on top after stirring and before returning to oven to finish baking. Cavatelli or campanelle pasta can be substituted for elbow macaroni.

S
I
D
E

D
I
S
H
E
S

Fryemont Inn Mushroom Business

½   pound mushrooms, sliced
2   tablespoons butter
½   cup chopped onion
½   cup diced green bell pepper
½   cup chopped celery
¼   teaspoon salt
    Dash freshly ground black
      pepper
¼   cup mayonnaise
6   slices crustless whole wheat
      bread
2   extra large eggs, beaten slightly
1   cup whole milk
1   14-ounce can cream of
      mushroom soup
1   cup grated Swiss or Monterey
      Jack cheese

Sauté mushrooms in butter, drain, remove and set aside. Combine chopped onion, green pepper, celery, salt, pepper, mayonnaise and sautéed mushrooms in a bowl. Mix well. Grease an 8-inch square casserole dish. Cut each bread slice into quarters. Lay half the pieces in the bottom of the casserole dish, overlapping slightly. Spread mushroom mixture evenly over bread. Top with remaining bread squares. In a small bowl, combine eggs and milk. Pour over bread slices. Cover and refrigerate 4 hours or overnight.

Preheat oven to 350°F. Spread undiluted soup over all. Bake 45 minutes. Sprinkle with cheese and bake an additional 10 minutes.

Serves 4

This dish has been served as a side dish at the Fryemont Inn in Bryson City, North Carolina, every Saturday night for over 25 years.

Onion Gratinée

12   medium onions,
        in ½-inch slices
9   tablespoons butter
6   tablespoons flour
     Pepper to taste
3   cups chicken broth
¾   cup sherry or white wine
3-4 cups unseasoned croutons
6   tablespoons grated
        Parmesan cheese
¾   cup grated Swiss cheese

Preheat oven to 350°F. Sauté onions in butter until tender. Add flour, pepper, broth, and sherry. Cook and stir over medium heat till thick and bubbly. Put in casserole dish and chill. Cover and bake for 30 minutes. Sprinkle with croutons and cheese. Bake 10 minutes more.

Serves 6-8

A number one request at every family holiday gathering. Double it for leftovers!

Mashed Potatoes Florentine

4   russet potatoes, washed, peeled and cubed
4   slices of bacon
2   green onions, minced
2⅓   cups milk
4   ounces crumbled blue cheese, divided
¼   cup softened butter
      Salt and freshly ground pepper
8   ounces fresh baby spinach, rinsed, drained, stems removed

Bring salted water to boil in 3-quart pot. Add cubed potatoes, boil until tender, about 20 minutes. Cook bacon in skillet over medium high heat until crisp, remove and drain, reserving drippings in skillet. Crumble bacon pieces. Add onions to skillet, and sauté until tender, remove from skillet. Drain cooked potatoes and place in stainless mixing bowl. Beat potatoes with electric mixer, gradually adding milk and 2 ounces of blue cheese. Add butter, salt and pepper to taste. Stir in bacon pieces and shallots. Keep warm. Sauté spinach in bacon drippings for 2 to 3 minutes or until just wilted. Remove from skillet and arrange spinach around edges of a serving plate. Ladle potatoes in center and sprinkle with remaining blue cheese.

Serves 6-8

This is an easy way to make mashed potatoes "special".

Sweet Potato Soufflé

5-6   medium sweet potatoes, peeled, boiled, and mashed
2   eggs, beaten
½   cup cream
⅓   cup brown sugar
1   teaspoon nutmeg
1   teaspoon cinnamon
½   teaspoon salt
½   cup raisins
1   tablespoon grated orange zest

Preheat oven to 350°F. In a medium sized bowl, mix potatoes, eggs and cream together. Add brown sugar, nutmeg, cinnamon, salt, raisins and orange zest. Place in buttered casserole and bake 25 minutes.

Serves 6-8

Parmesan Scalloped Potatoes

5   large baking potatoes, peeled and thinly sliced
¾   cup grated Parmesan cheese
3   tablespoons chopped fresh marjoram (1 tablespoon dried)
1   teaspoon salt
¾   teaspoon garlic powder
¼   teaspoon ground nutmeg
¼   teaspoon ground black pepper
3   cups whipping cream
¾   cup water
3   tablespoons grated Parmesan cheese
1½   tablespoons chopped fresh marjoram or 1½ teaspoons dried

Preheat oven to 350°F. Place potatoes in bowl of cool water. In a small bowl, combine ¾ cup Parmesan cheese, marjoram, salt, garlic powder, nutmeg, and pepper, set aside. In a lightly greased, shallow 3-quart baking dish, arrange ⅓ of potato slices, sprinkle with half of cheese mixture. Repeat layers with remaining potato slices and cheese mixture, ending with potato slices. Combine whipping cream and water, pour over top layer. Sprinkle with remaining cheese and marjoram. Cover and bake for 1½ hours. Uncover and bake an additional 30 minutes or until potato slices are tender. Let stand 10 minutes before serving.

Serves 12

Praline Sweet Potatoes

5   large sweet potatoes or yams
½   cup softened butter
½   cup sugar
2   eggs, beaten
1   teaspoon vanilla extract
⅓   cup milk
½   cup heavy cream
1   cup light brown sugar
1   cup chopped pecans

Preheat oven to 350°F. Scrub sweet potatoes and rub with small amount of cooking oil. Place on foil lined cookie sheet and bake until tender, about 45 minutes. Halve potatoes and scoop pulp into a large mixing bowl. Mash well. Mix softened butter into mashed potatoes along with the sugar, eggs, vanilla and milk, using electric mixer on low to medium speed. Spoon mixture into a 9x12-inch glass baking dish. Bring cream to a simmer in a small saucepan. Add brown sugar and stir until dissolved. Cook mixture over medium heat to soft ball stage (234°-240°F on candy thermometer). Remove from heat and beat in the butter and chopped pecans. Pour mixture over potatoes. Bake until very hot and beginning to brown.

Serves 6-8

Snow Peas with Hazelnuts

½ cup diced slab bacon
2 tablespoons butter
½ pound snow peas, washed
2 tablespoons chopped
  hazelnuts
Salt and pepper to taste

In a skillet, cook bacon over medium high heat, until just browned, about 6 minutes. Remove bacon from skillet and drain drippings. In same skillet, melt butter over low heat. Add snow peas and cook about 1 minute or until crisp tender. Add hazelnuts and cook, shaking the skillet occasionally, until golden. Add bacon, salt, and pepper and sauté 2 more minutes. Serve immediately.

Serves 2

S I D E   D I S H E S

Spinach and Bacon

4 thick slices bacon
2 garlic cloves, chopped
1 pound spinach, washed,
  stemmed, and drained
½ cup cooked navy beans,
  drained and rinsed
¼ teaspoon salt
¼ teaspoon pepper

In a large skillet over medium heat, cook bacon 10 minutes or until crisp. Remove bacon and drain, coarsely chop or crumble. Remove all but 1 tablespoon of bacon fat from skillet. Over medium heat, cook garlic 30 seconds, stirring constantly. Add spinach and beans. Cook until spinach is wilted, approximately 3 minutes. Season with salt and pepper. Transfer to serving dish with slotted spoon. Sprinkle bacon on top. Serve.

Serves 4

This dish can also be made using red Swiss chard instead of spinach.

Queso Style Spinach

4	10-ounce packages frozen chopped spinach
1-2	cups vegetable liquid (from cooking spinach)
½	stick butter
4	tablespoons flour
4	tablespoons minced onions
2	cloves garlic, minced
1	cup half-and-half
1	teaspoon black pepper
1	teaspoon white pepper
½	teaspoon hot red pepper sauce to taste
1	tablespoon Worcestershire sauce
12	ounces Mexican style processed cheese loaf, cubed
	Breadcrumbs (optional)

Preheat oven to 350°F. Cook spinach according to directions, then drain spinach and reserve liquid. Melt butter in a saucepan over low heat. Add flour, stirring until smooth but not brown. Add onions and garlic and cook until translucent. Add vegetable liquid slowly, stirring constantly to avoid lumps. Add half-and-half. Cook until thick and smooth, stirring. Add seasonings and cheese. Stir until melted, add in cooked spinach. Place in 9x13-inch casserole dish and top with breadcrumbs. Cook until bubbly.

Serves 6-8

A unique creamed spinach dish. The seasonings give it a nice "kick".

When sautéing, use a small amount
of chicken broth or wine instead of butter.

Simply Super Tomatoes

6	medium tomatoes, in ½-inch slices
⅔	cup vegetable oil
¼	cup wine vinegar
¼	cup finely chopped green onions
¼	cup finely chopped fresh parsley
1	garlic clove, minced
1	teaspoon salt
1	teaspoon dried dill weed
1	teaspoon dried basil leaves
¼	teaspoon pepper

Arrange tomatoes in glass or ceramic serving dish. In a small bowl or jar with lid, combine remaining ingredients, mix well. Pour dressing over tomatoes. Cover and refrigerate for 1 to 2 hours, periodically spooning dressing over tomatoes.

Serves 6-8

Autumn Vegetables with Bacon and Scallions

1½ pounds turnips, peeled and cut into 1-inch chunks

1 pound sweet potatoes, peeled and cut into 1-inch chunks

Salt

4 slices bacon

1 tablespoon unsalted butter, at room temperature

⅛ teaspoon ground cinnamon

¼ teaspoon pepper

2 scallions, thinly sliced

In a large saucepan, put turnips, sweet potatoes, and cold water to cover, salt generously. Cover and bring to a boil over high heat, then reduce heat to medium low and simmer until very tender, 10 to 12 minutes. Drain. Beat with an electric mixer or mash with a potato masher until fairly smooth. Cook bacon in a skillet until crisp. Reserve drippings. Drain bacon and crumble coarsely. Add butter and bacon drippings to vegetables. Stir in cinnamon and pepper. Spoon into a serving dish and top with scallions and bacon.

Serves 8

S I D E   D I S H E S

Roasted Summer Vegetables

3 large tomatoes, sliced

1 large sweet onion

2 medium zucchini, sliced

2 medium yellow squash, sliced

2 cloves garlic, minced

3 tablespoons olive oil

1 tablespoon sweet basil

Salt and pepper to taste

½ cup grated Parmesan cheese

Preheat oven to 375°F. Slice tomatoes and arrange in baking dish. In a medium sized bowl, toss onion, zucchini, squash, and garlic in oil. Arrange tossed vegetables over tomatoes. Sprinkle with basil, salt and pepper to taste. Top with grated Parmesan cheese. Cover with foil. Bake 45-60 minutes depending on degree of doneness preferred.

Serves 4-6

Oven-Fried Turnips

4   turnips, trimmed and peeled
      (about 1¼ pounds)
2   tablespoons olive oil
1   teaspoon kosher salt
1   teaspoon chili powder

Heat oven to 425°F. Cut turnips into french fry size sticks. Combine oil, salt and chili powder into a large plastic storage bag. Add turnips and shake well to thoroughly coat. Place turnips on a foil lined pan in a single layer. Roast 20-30 minutes, turning halfway through cooking time for even browning. Serve immediately.

Serves 6

These are amazingly good, even for those who don't like turnips.

167

Zucchini and Fresh Mozzarella

3   zucchini (about 1 pound), cut
      lengthwise into ¼-inch slices
2   tablespoons olive oil
¼   teaspoon salt
⅛   teaspoon freshly ground black
      pepper
¼   teaspoon wine vinegar
1   clove garlic, minced
1   tablespoon chopped flat-leaf
      parsley
½   pound fresh mozzarella, cut
      into thick slices

Preheat oven to broil or heat outdoor grill. In a large glass or stainless steel bowl, toss zucchini with 1 tablespoon of oil, salt, and pepper. Grill or broil zucchini, turning once, until tender and golden, about 5 minutes per side. Return zucchini to bowl, toss with ½ tablespoon oil, vinegar, garlic, and parsley. Cool. Arrange mozzarella slices in a circle on a serving plate. Drizzle cheese with the remaining ½ tablespoon oil and sprinkle with a pinch of pepper. Fold the zucchini slices in half and tuck them between the pieces of cheese.

Serves 4

The delicate taste of fresh mozzarella is a delicious counterpoint to the garlic-vinegar macerated zucchini.

For a stronger cheese flavor, substitute goat cheese for mozzarella.

S
I
D
E

D
I
S
H
E
S

Baked Zucchini and Tomatoes with Feta

6	small zucchini, sliced
1	can diced tomatoes, with juice
½	teaspoon dried oregano
½	teaspoon chopped garlic
¼	cup dry white wine
2	tablespoons chopped fresh parsley
1	2.25-ounce can sliced black olives
2	ounces crumbled feta cheese

Preheat oven to 350°F. Put zucchini in large pot and barely cover with salted water. Bring to a boil, reduce heat and simmer until just tender. Drain well. In a large bowl, toss drained zucchini with tomatoes. Pour into a greased casserole dish.

Combine oregano, garlic, wine and parsley. Pour over zucchini and tomato mixture. Sprinkle olives over all. Bake 20-25 minutes. Serve with feta crumbled over the top.

Serves 4

A classic from the Fryemont Inn in Bryson City, North Carolina.

S
I
D
E

D
I
S
H
E
S

Preserve the flavor of fresh herbs by making herb butter. Let butter soften, then add finely chopped herbs in any combination, about 2 to 4 tablespoons per stick of butter. The butter freezes well, and can be served on French bread or with seafood or chicken.

BREAD & BREAKFAST

Contents

Hot Curried Fruit Compote

1   15.5-ounce can pineapple chunks
1   16-ounce can peach slices
1   16-ounce can pear slices
1   8.5-ounce can apricot halves
1   14.25-ounce can pitted dark sweet cherries
2   tablespoons butter
     Splash of either rum or brandy (optional)
¾   cup brown sugar
1   tablespoon Madras curry powder
     Walnuts (optional)

Preheat oven to 325°F. Drain fruit and arrange in a glass or ceramic baking dish. Dot fruit with butter and sprinkle with rum or brandy. In a separate bowl, combine brown sugar and curry powder. Sprinkle evenly over the fruit. Bake 30-45 minutes. Sprinkle with nuts and serve warm.

Serves 8

Easy to make, a great dish for a brunch or holiday guests.

Madras curry powder is extremely spicy hot. Regular curry powder or a combination of Madras and regular curry powder may be substituted. Decrease the amount of curry powder for a milder flavor.

Granola

5   cups oats
1   cup soy nuts
1   cup chopped almonds
1   cup sunflower seeds
1   cup powdered milk
¼   cup brown sugar
1   cup wheat germ
1   cup flour
1   cup oil
1   cup honey
1   cup raisins
1   cup dates, chopped

Preheat oven to 200°F. Mix first 4 ingredients. Add dry ingredients. Mix with oil and honey. Layer on a lightly greased cookie sheet or in 2 9x13-inch pans. Bake 40 minutes. Add raisins and dates and bake 20 more minutes. Cool. Keeps well in an airtight container. Other dried fruits and nuts can be substituted.

Potato and Herb Frittata

8 large eggs
¼ teaspoon salt
½ teaspoon black pepper
¼ cup olive oil
2 cups frozen shredded hash brown potatoes (from 16-ounce bag)
1 bunch scallions, chopped
1 5-ounce package garlic herb cheese

Preheat oven to 375°F; place oven rack in middle position. Whisk together eggs, salt, and pepper until just combined. Heat oil in an ovenproof 9 or 10-inch, heavy-duty nonstick skillet over high heat until very hot but not smoking. Add potatoes and scallions to oil, stirring once, then cover and cook until beginning to brown, about 4 minutes. Stir and flip potato mixture once, cover and cook 3 more minutes. Pour eggs over potato mixture and crumble cheese over eggs. Transfer skillet to oven and bake frittata, uncovered, until set and just cooked through, about 15 minutes. Invert a plate over skillet, holding them together with oven mitts, then invert frittata onto plate. Serve immediately.

Serves 4

B
R
E
A
D

&

B
R
E
A
K
F
A
S
T

Turkey Quiche

1 box of seasoned stuffing mix
1 cup cooked turkey, chopped
1 cup Swiss cheese, shredded (or cheese of your choice)
4 eggs
1 5-ounce can evaporated milk
⅛ teaspoon pepper

Preheat oven to 400°F. Prepare stuffing according to package directions. Press stuffing into a lightly greased 9-inch pie pan. Bake 10 minutes. Sprinkle meat and cheese into hot crust. Beat eggs, milk, and pepper together and pour on top of meat and cheese. Lower heat to 350°F and bake for 30-35 minutes or until center is set.

Serves 4

This recipe is great at any altitude! A great way to use leftover holiday turkey, makes a quick meal, and is an easy recipe for potlucks!

Potato and Egg Strata

12	eggs
1	cup plain yogurt
1	teaspoon seasoned salt
¾	stick butter
¼	cup (or less) chopped onion
2	cups thawed, shredded hash brown potatoes
1	cup grated sharp Cheddar cheese

Preheat oven to 350°F. Spray or grease a two-quart casserole dish with cooking oil. Beat eggs, yogurt, and salt together. Melt butter and lightly sauté onion. Add thawed potatoes. Stir to mix. Pour in egg mixture and lightly stir to blend ingredients. Pour into casserole dish. Sprinkle grated cheese over casserole. Bake approximately 25 minutes or until knife comes out clean when inserted. Cut into 8 squares. May be prepared the night before and refrigerated overnight. Bring to room temperature before baking.

Serves 8

Great for overnight guests. Wrap precooked sausages in aluminum foil and heat on the same rack. Broil a dozen English muffins while plating the casserole and sausages. Makes a hearty breakfast with little mess and easy timing to get everything warm to the table.

Quick Shrimp Quiche

1	tube crescent dinner roll refrigerated dough
1	pound shrimp, shelled and deveined
12	thin slices of pepperoni, shredded
2	tablespoons butter
1	pimento, slivered
1½	cups grated Swiss cheese
4	eggs
1¾	cups light cream
	Pinch of salt, pepper, and dry mustard

Preheat oven to 400°F. Grease a 13x9x2-inch baking dish and cover bottom with rectangles of crescent roll dough, pressing firmly to seal all seams. Sauté shrimp and pepperoni lightly in butter and add pimento. Sprinkle cheese on dough crust. Top with shrimp mixture. Beat eggs with remaining ingredients and pour into crust. Bake at 400°F for 10 minutes. Reduce heat to 325°F and bake for 40 minutes or until custard is set.

Serves 6

A 6-ounce package of defrosted frozen shrimp may be substituted for fresh shrimp. Add some chopped onions for a different flavor and, of course, hot pepper sauce! This recipe has been adjusted for 8,000-9,000 feet altitude.

Spinach, Sausage, and Cheese Breakfast Quiche

2   10-ounce boxes of frozen chopped spinach
2   tablespoons olive oil
2   tablespoons chopped garlic
1   cup chopped onions
1   cup diced green, red, or yellow peppers (or a combination)
1   cup finely sliced celery
½   cup chopped sun-dried tomatoes
4   eggs
1   2-pound container of ricotta cheese
½   teaspoon of nutmeg
2   tablespoons Creole seasoning (or other seasoning salt)
2   tablespoons dill weed
8   ounces shredded Parmesan cheese (or sharp Cheddar)

Preheat oven to 375°F. Grease 9x13-inch baking dish with vegetable oil spray. Defrost spinach, drain, and squeeze dry. Heat olive oil in skillet and lightly sauté garlic, onions, peppers, and celery. Add sun-dried tomatoes and set aside to cool. In a large bowl, beat eggs and then gradually add ricotta and seasonings, mixing well. Gradually add vegetable mixture to ricotta mixture, stirring after each addition to evenly distribute vegetable pieces. Pour into oil-sprayed casserole dish and press evenly with the back of a large spoon. Sprinkle Parmesan evenly over casserole. Bake 45-50 minutes or until top is golden brown. Serve hot or at room temperature.

Serves 8-12

Italian sausage or ground round may be added. Be sure to sauté and drain grease before adding to casserole.

Pancakes are lighter and fluffier when club soda is substituted for milk in the batter. Instead of milk, try buttermilk, yogurt or sour cream. It can add a whole new flavor and improve nutrition.

Bed and Breakfast Blueberry Pancakes

4	tablespoons butter
1	cup flour
½	teaspoon salt
½	teaspoon baking powder
½	teaspoon baking soda
1	cup plain or vanilla yogurt
2	eggs
¼	cup milk
1	cup blueberries, washed and drained well

Melt butter and set aside. Mix dry ingredients in a separate bowl. Add yogurt and eggs to dry ingredients and beat until blended. Add melted butter and milk and beat until batter is smooth. Ladle batter onto a hot griddle according to the size of pancakes you prefer. Sprinkle blueberries on top on the raw side. When small bubbles appear on the surface, flip and finish cooking. Serve with warm maple syrup and/or powdered sugar.

Serves 6-8

This recipe is from a New England Bed and Breakfast. These pancakes are like no other homemade pancakes!

Sparkling Cider Pancakes with Apple Cider Syrup

2½	cups pancake mix
½	cup quick oatmeal
½	teaspoon cinnamon
1	cup cold water
½	cup sparkling cider

APPLE CIDER SYRUP

¾	cup apple cider
½	cup packed brown sugar
½	cup light corn syrup
2	tablespoons butter
½	teaspoon lemon juice
⅛	teaspoon cinnamon
⅛	teaspoon nutmeg

Pancakes: Blend together all ingredients using a wire whisk. For thicker pancakes, allow batter to sit for 5 minutes. Cook pancakes on a hot oiled griddle until golden brown, turning to cook other side when pancakes have a bubbly surface and slightly dry edges. Serve with warm apple cider syrup.

Apple Cider Syrup: In a small saucepan, mix all ingredients. Bring to boil over medium-high heat, stirring occasionally. Reduce heat and simmer, uncovered, for 15-20 minutes or until thickened.

Serves 4

BREAD & BREAKFAST

Whole Wheat Pancakes

⅔ cup unbleached flour
½ cup whole wheat flour
2 tablespoons sugar
2 teaspoons baking powder
¼ teaspoon salt
1 egg beaten
⅔ cup milk
2 tablespoons margarine

In a medium bowl mix the dry ingredients and add the egg, milk, and margarine. Cook pancakes on a hot grill until golden brown, turning to cook other side when pancakes have a bubbly surface and slightly dry edges. Serve immediately.

Serves 4

ORANGE BLOSSOM HONEY BUTTER
½ cup orange blossom honey
¼ cup butter, softened
¼ teaspoon grated orange zest
¼ teaspoon grated lemon zest

Combine all ingredients in a medium bowl. Beat until blended (about 2 minutes). Refrigerate until ready to use. (2¼ teaspoons per serving.)

Serves 16

Delicious on homemade biscuits, pancakes, or waffles.

Baked Blueberry French Toast

1 whole loaf day-old French bread
5 eggs
4 tablespoons sugar
1 teaspoon vanilla extract
2½ cups milk

TOPPING
½ cup flour
6 tablespoons dark brown sugar
½ teaspoon cinnamon
¼ cup butter or margarine
1 cup fresh or frozen blueberries, rinsed and drained
1 cup sliced strawberries

Preheat oven to 375°F. Grease 13x9-inch baking dish. Cut bread diagonally into 1-inch slices and place in baking dish and set aside. In medium bowl, lightly beat eggs, sugar, and vanilla. Stir in milk until well blended. Pour mixture over bread in baking dish, turning slices to coat well. Cover and refrigerate overnight.

Topping: In small bowl, combine flour, brown sugar, and cinnamon. Cut in butter or margarine until mixture resembles coarse crumbs. Scatter blueberries over bread and sprinkle evenly with crumb mixture. Bake about 50 minutes or until golden brown and the egg mixture is well set. Before serving, cut into squares and top with strawberries. Serve with syrup, yogurt, or as is.

Serves 8

Great for Easter Brunch or a special breakfast for guests.

Night-Before French Toast Casserole

1	8-10-ounce baguette, cut in 1-inch slices
6	large eggs
2½	cups whole milk
4	teaspoons sugar
¾	teaspoon salt
1	tablespoon vanilla
1	ounce orange juice
2	tablespoons butter, cut in tiny pieces

Grease a 9x13-inch baking pan with butter or vegetable cooking spray. Arrange bread slices in a single layer. In a large bowl, beat eggs with milk, sugar, salt, vanilla, and orange juice. Pour over bread in pan. Cover with foil and refrigerate at least 4 hours or up to 36 hours. To bake, uncover pan and dot with butter pieces. Put pan in cold oven. Preheat oven to 350°F and bake 45-60 minutes, until bread is puffy and lightly browned. Remove from oven and let stand 5 minutes before serving. Serve with syrup, honey, yogurt, or sour cream and fresh fruit.

Serves 8

Knock-Your-Socks-Off Waffles

2	cups flour
½	teaspoon salt
4	teaspoons baking powder
2	tablespoons sugar
2	eggs
1½	cups warm milk
⅓	cup melted butter
1	teaspoon vanilla extract
	Toasted chopped pecans (optional)

For this recipe it is essential to add ingredients in the order listed. In a large bowl, mix together flour, salt, baking powder, and sugar. Set aside. In a separate bowl, beat the eggs well. Stir in the milk, butter, and vanilla. Pour the milk mixture into the flour mixture. Beat until blended. If desired, add pecans to batter. Ladle the batter into a preheated waffle iron and cook until golden and crisp. Serve immediately.

Serves 4-8

Batter can also be easily made in a sturdy blender.

Onion Lover's Twist

1   package dry yeast
¼   cup warm water
4   cups flour
¼   cup sugar
½   cup hot water
½   cup milk
¼   cup margarine or softened
       butter
1   egg

FILLING

¼   cup butter or margarine
1   cup finely chopped onion, (or
       ¼ cup instant minced onions)
1   tablespoon grated Parmesan
       cheese
1   tablespoon sesame or poppy
       seeds
¼   teaspoon garlic powder
¼   teaspoon salt
1   teaspoon paprika

Grease a cookie sheet. Dissolve yeast in warm water in a large bowl. Add 2 cups flour, sugar, salt, water, milk, butter, and egg. With electric mixer, blend at low speed until moistened. Beat 2 minutes at medium speed. By hand, stir in remaining flour to form soft dough. Cover and let rise in a warm place until light and doubled in size, approximately 45-60 minutes. Filling: melt butter in saucepan and add remaining ingredients.

Preheat oven to 350°F. When dough has doubled in size, stir down and place on a floured board. Knead until no longer sticky. Roll out to an 18x12-inch rectangle. Cut lengthwise into three 18x4-inch strips. Spread filling down the middle of each strip. Beginning with the long side, roll up each strip and seal edges. (Edges are hard to seal if butter gets on them.) On the prepared cookie sheet, braid the three rolls together. Cover and allow to rise until doubled, about 45-60 minutes. Brush egg white on the top and sprinkle with sesame or poppy seeds. Bake for 30-35 minutes, or until golden brown.

Makes 1 loaf

This recipe has been prepared successfully at an altitude of 7,000 feet.

B
R
E
A
D

&

B
R
E
A
K
F
A
S
T

Apple Harvest Coffee Cake

1½ cups sugar
1 cup flour
2 teaspoons baking powder
½ teaspoon salt
1 teaspoon vanilla
2 eggs
2 cups peeled, chopped apples
1 cup chopped walnuts

Preheat oven to 350°F. Stir together sugar, flour, baking powder, and salt. Beat eggs and vanilla and add to dry ingredients. Mix well. Fold in apples and walnuts. Put in a greased 9-inch pie plate (or something comparable). Bake for 25-30 minutes (a little longer at higher altitudes). Serve hot with whipped cream.

Serves 4-6

This is an old Maine recipe that has been passed down a couple of generations. Makes a great dessert when served with ice cream.

Banana Coffee Cake

¼ cup butter
1½ cups sugar
2 eggs
3 bananas, mashed
5 tablespoons milk
1 tablespoon vanilla
2 cups flour
1 teaspoon baking soda

TOPPING
6 tablespoons melted butter
1 cup brown sugar
1 cup chopped nuts

Preheat oven to 350°F. Grease a 9x13-inch pan. Cream together butter and sugar. Add eggs and mix well. Mix in bananas, milk, and vanilla. Add flour and baking soda and mix well. Pour into prepared pan. For topping, mix together butter, sugar, and nuts. Spoon topping mixture on top of batter. Bake 35-45 minutes.

Serves 12-24

This recipe has been successfully prepared at an altitude of 7,500 feet.

Reen's Great Depression Cake

2 cups hot apple juice
2 tablespoons decaffeinated coffee
1 4-ounce stick butter
2 cups raisins
1 large or 2 small apples, peeled and grated
2 cups plus 3 tablespoons all-purpose flour
1 teaspoon baking powder
1 teaspoon each: cinnamon, all spice, ground cloves, ground nutmeg
1 cup broken walnuts

Preheat oven to 350°F. Grease 9x13-inch pan (or 4 small loaf pans). Mix and simmer first 4 ingredients for 10 minutes. Cool 10-15 minutes. Mix final 6 ingredients and add to cooled liquid. Pour into greased 9x13-inch pan or 4 small loaf pans. Cook 25-30 minutes or until wooden toothpick inserted in center of cake comes out clean. Cool, cut, and serve.

Serves 8-12

This recipe has been baked at an elevation of 6,200 feet.

Orange Coconut Crescents

1 8-ounce tube refrigerated crescent dinner roll dough
2 tablespoons softened butter or margarine
⅓ cup flaked coconut
⅓ cup sugar
1 tablespoon grated orange zest

GLAZE
¼ cup sugar
¼ cup sour cream
2 tablespoons orange juice
2 tablespoons butter or margarine

Preheat oven to 375°F. Separate crescent rolls and spread with butter. In a bowl, combine coconut, sugar, and orange zest. Set aside 2 tablespoons for topping. Sprinkle remaining coconut mixture over butter. Roll up and place pointed side down on a greased baking sheet. Bake for 16-18 minutes or until golden brown. Meanwhile, combine glaze ingredients in a saucepan. Bring to a boil and boil for 3 minutes or until mixture is glossy. Cool slightly. Pour over warm rolls. Sprinkle with remaining reserved coconut mixture.

Serves 4- 8

These rich rolls are perfect for brunch when served with fresh fruit and coffee.

Blueberry Scones

¾ cup blueberries, rinsed and dried
1¾ cups sifted flour
2¼ teaspoons baking powder
2 tablespoons sugar, divided
½ teaspoon salt
¼ cup softened butter
2 eggs, beaten
⅓ cup cream

Preheat oven to 450°F. Place blueberries in small colander. Rinse and then drain on paper towels. In large bowl, mix together flour, baking powder, 1 tablespoon sugar, and salt. Cut in butter, using a pastry blender. In separate bowl, beat eggs. (Add 1 teaspoon water per egg for altitude cooking.) Reserve 2 tablespoons of egg mixture and add rest to dry ingredients. Pour in cream. Combine with a few quick strokes, then gently fold in blueberries using spatula. Place on a slightly floured board and pat or roll to ¾-inch thickness. Cut into diamond shapes or 2-inch rounds. Brush with reserved egg and sprinkle with remaining sugar. Bake 15 minutes.

Serves 6

Bake these on a stone cookie pan - they will come out perfect!

Good-for-Your-Health Apple Cinnamon Muffins

¼ cup canola oil
¼ cup maple syrup
1 cup applesauce
1½ cups whole wheat pastry flour
2 tablespoons ground flax seed
½ teaspoon baking soda
1 teaspoon baking powder
¾ teaspoon cinnamon
1 pinch sea salt
½ cup walnuts, chopped

Preheat oven to 375°F. Grease 12 muffin cups or line with paper liners. Combine oil, maple syrup, and applesauce in a medium size bowl. Stir to mix. In a separate bowl, sift together flour, ground flaxseed, baking soda, baking powder, cinnamon, and salt. Stir in walnuts. Combine wet and dry ingredients. Stir until just combined. Use a large spoon to drop the muffin batter into the muffin tins. Bake for 18-20 minutes.

Makes 12 muffins.

A healthy, tasty recipe that has been prepared at an altitude of 8,500 feet.

Sweetness-and-Light Banana Date Muffin Cakes

1¾	cups unbleached all-purpose flour
½	cup sugar
1½	teaspoons baking powder
¼	teaspoon salt
¼	teaspoon freshly grated nutmeg
½	teaspoon cinnamon
1	teaspoon grated lemon zest
½	cup milk
⅓	cup melted butter
1	large egg, lightly beaten
1	teaspoon vanilla extract
2	mashed bananas
⅔	cup diced, pitted dates

Preheat oven to 400°F. Grease 12 muffin cups or line with paper liners. In large mixing bowl, combine flour, sugar, baking powder, salt, nutmeg, cinnamon, and lemon zest. In a second bowl, whisk together milk, butter, egg, and vanilla. Add wet ingredients to the dry and combine with as few strokes as possible. Fold in bananas and dates. Spoon batter into prepared muffin cups, filling each one ½-⅔ full. Bake until golden brown, 15-20 minutes. If using miniature muffin tins, bake for 10 minutes.

Makes 12 muffins.

Strawberry Pecan Muffins

2	cups flour
¼	cup sugar
2	teaspoons baking powder
1	teaspoon lemon zest
¼	teaspoon salt
⅔	cup milk
¼	cup melted butter or margarine
1	egg
2	cups finely chopped strawberries

STREUSEL TOPPING

¼	cup flour
¼	cup finely chopped pecans
¼	cup light brown sugar
2	tablespoons softened butter or margarine

Preheat oven to 400°F. In large bowl combine flour, sugar, baking powder, lemon zest, and salt. In another bowl whisk together milk, melted butter, and egg until blended. Make a well in center of flour mixture; pour in liquid and stir until just moistened. Do not over-mix. The batter will be lumpy. Fold in strawberries. Spoon batter into greased muffin tin, filling ⅔ full.

Streusel Topping: Combine all ingredients, mixing until crumbly. Sprinkle topping over muffins. Bake 20-25 minutes.

Makes 16 muffins.

Very pretty and not too sweet. This recipe has been adjusted for an altitude of 9,100 feet.

Cranberry Bread

1 cup whole wheat flour
1 cup all-purpose flour
½-⅔ cup sugar, to taste
1½ teaspoons baking powder
½ teaspoon baking soda
½ teaspoon salt (optional)
3 tablespoons vegetable oil
4 teaspoons grated orange zest
¾ cup fresh orange juice
1 egg
1⅓ cups coarsely chopped fresh cranberries
½ cup chopped nuts

Preheat oven to 350°F. Grease a 9x5-inch loaf pan (or 2 smaller ones). In a large bowl, stir together whole wheat and all-purpose flour, sugar, baking powder, baking soda, and salt. In a small bowl, whisk together oil, orange zest, orange juice, and egg. Add this mixture to the flour mixture, stirring until just moist. Fold in the cranberries and nuts. Pour batter into prepared pan. Bake 1 hour. Cool on wire rack 10 minutes. Remove from pan and cool completely. Wrap bread well and let stand overnight before slicing. If using smaller pans, bake about 30-35 minutes.

Makes 1 large loaf or 2 small loaves.

This recipe has been prepared at an altitude of 8,500 feet.

Zucchini Chocolate Nut Bread

3 eggs
2 cups sugar, less 4 tablespoons
1 cup plus 3 tablespoons vegetable oil
1 teaspoon vanilla
2 cups grated zucchini
2 ounces melted, unsweetened chocolate
2 cups flour
1 teaspoon baking soda
1 teaspoon salt
1 teaspoon cinnamon
1 cup chopped walnuts or pecans
½ cup chocolate chips

Preheat oven to 350°F. Grease two mid-sized loaf pans. In a large bowl, beat eggs until pale yellow. While beating, gradually add sugar, oil, and vanilla. Stir in zucchini and melted chocolate. Mix dry ingredients. Gradually add to zucchini mixture, stirring after each addition. Stir in nuts and chocolate chips. Pour into prepared pans. Bake for 1 hour or until a wooden toothpick inserted in the middle comes out clean.

Makes 2 loaves.

Serve small slices. It has a rich chocolate flavor and smooth texture. Also makes a great dessert.

Blueberry Lemon Bread

⅓   cup plus 1 tablespoon butter
1   cup sugar
2   eggs
1½ cups all-purpose flour
1   teaspoon baking powder
    Pinch of salt
½   cup milk
2   teaspoons grated lemon zest
1   cup fresh blueberries
2   teaspoons all-purpose flour

Preheat oven to 350°F. With electric mixer, cream butter. Gradually add sugar, beating at medium speed until well blended. Add eggs, one at a time, beating well after each addition. Combine flour, baking powder, and salt. Add to creamed mixture alternating with milk, beginning and ending with flour mixture. Stir in lemon zest. Dredge blueberries in 2 teaspoons flour and fold into batter. Pour batter into a greased 8x4x3-inch loaf pan. Bake for 55 minutes or until wooden pick inserted in center comes out clean. Cool bread in the pan for 30 minutes. Brush top with melted butter.

Makes 1 loaf.

This recipe has been successfully prepared and doubled at an altitude of 7,500 feet.

In a pinch, you may substitute orange zest for lemon zest.

BREAD & BREAKFAST

High altitude has its most pronounced effect on the rising time of bread.

Miniature Pumpkin Breads

Nonstick vegetable oil spray

3 cups raw pumpkin seeds (pepitas, about 15 ounces)

3½ cups unbleached all-purpose flour

2 teaspoons baking powder

2 teaspoons baking soda

1½ teaspoons salt

1½ teaspoons ground cinnamon

¼ teaspoon ground nutmeg

3 cups canned pure pumpkin

1 cup sugar

1 cup packed golden brown sugar

1 cup vegetable oil

4 large eggs

1 teaspoon peeled and minced fresh ginger

¾ cup buttermilk

Preheat oven to 350°F. Spray six miniature loaf pans with nonstick cooking spray. Spread seeds out on rimmed baking sheet. Roast seeds about 20 minutes, stirring twice, until beginning to color. Cool seeds. Set aside ½ cup whole seeds for topping. Coarsely grind remaining seeds by pulsing in food processor.

Combine flour, baking powder, baking soda, salt, cinnamon, and nutmeg in medium bowl. Whisk to blend. Mix in ground pumpkin seeds. Using electric mixer, beat pure pumpkin and both sugars in large bowl until blended. Gradually beat in oil, then eggs one at a time. Add ginger. Stir dry ingredients in 4 additions alternately with buttermilk in 3 additions. Divide batter among prepared pans. Sprinkle with reserved ½ cup whole pumpkin seeds. Bake breads 1 hour or until wooden toothpick inserted in center comes out clean. Cool in pans. Cover and store at room temperature.

Makes 6 miniature loaves.

These loaves freeze very well. Pumpkin seeds are available in bulk at natural health food stores.

Remove top oven rack to prevent cake from sticking to it, since high altitude cakes rise higher.

Buttermilk Banana Bread

7	tablespoons soft butter
¾	cup sugar
2	beaten eggs or 4 beaten egg whites
3	ripe bananas
1	teaspoon vanilla extract
1¾	cups flour
1	teaspoon baking soda
6	tablespoons buttermilk
1	cup nuts, chopped (optional)

Preheat oven to 325°F. Lightly grease a standard loaf pan or 3 miniature loaf pans. Cream butter and sugar. Add beaten eggs. Mash bananas. Add bananas and vanilla. In separate bowl, mix flour and soda and add to mixture. Add buttermilk (or add ¼ teaspoon white vinegar to 6 tablespoons milk as a substitute for buttermilk). Pour mixture into prepared pan(s). Bake 1 hour for a large loaf 40-45 minutes for miniature loaves.

Makes 1 loaf or 3 miniature loaves

This is a family favorite. The recipe has been adapted for high-altitude baking.

Thunder Ridge Cinnamon Rolls

2	cups flour
1	18-ounce package yellow cake mix
1	package dry yeast
1	cup hot water
2	tablespoons soft margarine
1	teaspoon cinnamon
3	tablespoons brown sugar

GLAZE

¼	pound powdered sugar
¼	cup butter or margarine, melted
2½	tablespoons milk
1	teaspoon vanilla or maple flavoring

Mix flour, cake mix, yeast, and water until well blended, and mixture is a smooth dough. Cover with wax paper and a clean towel. Set in a warm spot and let rise until double in size, about 2 hours. Roll out to 1-inch thickness. Spread with softened butter. Sprinkle with brown sugar and cinnamon. Roll up in jelly roll fashion. Cut into 12 equal pieces (to cut, place a piece of thread or dental floss under the roll and pull up through roll). Place on greased cookie sheet. Cover and refrigerate overnight. The following morning, preheat oven to 350°F. Place rolls in oven and bake 20-25 minutes. To make the glaze, in a small bowl whisk together all glaze ingredients. When done, drizzle glaze over warm rolls.

Makes 12 rolls

Lemony Lemon Bread

½	cup vegetable shortening
1	cup sugar
2	eggs
1¾	cups all-purpose flour
1	teaspoon baking powder
½	teaspoon of salt
½	cup milk
1	tablespoon finely grated lemon zest
½	cup chopped pecans
	Lemon syrup
¼	cup sugar
3	tablespoons fresh lemon juice

Preheat oven to 350°F. Grease and flour a medium loaf pan. In a large bowl, combine shortening and sugar and beat until blended. Add one egg at a time, beating well after each addition. In a medium bowl, mix together flour, baking powder, and salt. Add to shortening mixture, along with milk and lemon zest. Beat until blended and smooth. Stir in pecans. Spread evenly in prepared pan. Bake 1 hour or until a wooden toothpick inserted in center comes out clean.

Lemon syrup: Combine sugar and lemon juice in a small bowl. Set aside, stirring occasionally. (Sugar may not dissolve completely.) When bread is done, remove from oven and, using a fork or wooden toothpick, gently poke the top in several places. Stir the syrup, then slowly drizzle it over the hot bread. Cool in the pan for 15 minutes, then turn out onto a wire rack to cool completely.

Makes 1 loaf.

Baked successfully at an altitude of 8,500 feet.

Bread Machine Wheat Bread

1¼	cups hot water
½	cup oil
½	cup honey
4¾	cups freshly milled wheat flour
2	teaspoons salt
1	tablespoon yeast

Add ingredients in the order specified for bread machine. Set bread machine accordingly. When tested, this recipe came out perfect at a setting for a 2-pound wheat bread loaf.

Makes 1 loaf.

Use a wheat flour made for high-altitude baking. This bread was successfully prepared at an altitude of 8,500 feet.

Two-Loaf Whole Wheat Bread

2¾	cups warm water
3½	cups whole wheat flour
⅛	cup honey
⅛	cup molasses
⅛	cup oil
1½	tablespoons yeast
1	tablespoon dough enhancer
1	tablespoon salt
4-5	cups whole wheat flour

Preheat oven to 350°F. In an electric stand mixer with a dough hook attachment, mix water, flour, honey, molasses, oil, yeast and dough enhancer; let sit about 10 minutes until bubbly (sponge phase). With mixer on low, add 1 tablespoon of salt and enough flour to clean the sides of the bowl (approximately 4 or more cups). Knead dough 5-10 minutes (about 10 minutes by hand and 5-8 minutes if using a mixer).

Place dough into greased bread pans or free form and place on greased baking tray. Cover with tea towel and let rise until doubled. Bake 30-40 minutes or until bread sounds hollow when tapped.

Makes 2 loaves.

If desired, use all honey instead of honey and molasses.

Use a wheat flour made for high-altitude baking. This bread was successfully prepared at an altitude of 8,500 feet.

At high altitudes the rising period is shortened. Since the development of a good flavor in bread partially depends on the length of the rising period, it is well to maintain that period. Punching the dough down twice gives time for the flavor to develop.

Ezekiel Bread

7	cups whole grain wheat
1	cup whole grain barley
¼	cup dried pinto beans
¼	cup dried soy beans
¼	dried lentils
1	cup rye
5	cups warm water
½	cup softened butter
½	cup molasses or honey
3	tablespoons yeast
½	cup millet
1½	teaspoons salt
½	cup gluten

Preheat oven to 350°F. Combine first six ingredients in a grain mill to make a flour mixture. In an electric stand mixer with a dough hook attachment, combine warm water, butter, molasses, and yeast. Let sponge (sit until bubbly for 5 minutes). Add millet, milled flour, salt, and gluten until dough pulls away from the sides of the bowl. Knead for 7-8 minutes. Shape into 4 round loaves or place in bread pans. Let rise. Bake 30-35 minutes or until bread sounds hollow when tapped.

Makes 4 loaves.

This is a FANTASTIC bread, moist and packed with protein. A great way to incorporate beans into your diet! This bread will not rise as high as "regular" wheat bread.

For a smoother texture, add millet when making flour mixture. Wheat, barley, beans, lentils and rye may be purchased pre-ground into flour at a health food market.

189

B R E A D & B R E A K F A S T

In addition, flours tend to be drier and thus able to absorb more liquid in high, dry climates. Therefore, less flour may be needed to make the dough the proper consistency.

Flax Seed Bread

4 cups flax seed milled in the blender
5½ cups warm water
½ cup oil
½ cup honey
3 tablespoons yeast
3 tablespoons dough enhancer
2 cups whole wheat flour
1 tablespoon salt
6-8 cups whole wheat flour

Preheat oven to 350°F. In an electric stand mixer with a dough hook attachment, combine the first 7 ingredients until moistened and let sit for 10-15 minutes (sponge phase) until bubbly. Add 1 tablespoon salt and enough whole wheat flour to clean the sides of the bowl. Dough should feel tacky, not sticky. Knead for 5 minutes. Place in lightly greased loaf pans or free-form into rounds, cover with tea towel, and let rise. Bake 35 minutes or until bread sounds hollow when tapped.

Makes 4 loaves

Above 5000 feet, less yeast is required for most recipes. You will need to experiment with individual recipes, but general guide lines are:

White and Whole Wheat at 7500 feet
1st rising: 45 minutes
2nd rising: 25 minutes
Pan rising: 25 minutes

Sweet Coffee Cakes
1st rising: 55 minutes
Pan rising: 35 minutes

DESSERTS

Contents

Amaretto Chocolate Cake

CAKE

¾	cup slivered almonds
1	19-ounce chocolate cake mix
1	4½-ounce package instant chocolate pudding mix
4	eggs
½	cup cold water
½	cup vegetable oil
½	cup amaretto liqueur

GLAZE

4	tablespoons butter (½ stick)
2	tablespoons water
½	cup granulated sugar
¼	cup amaretto liqueur

Cake: Preheat oven to 325°F. Grease and flour 10-inch tube or 12-cup Bundt pan. Sprinkle nuts over bottom of pan. Combine the cake mix, pudding mix, eggs, water, oil, and liqueur and mix well. Pour batter over nuts. Bake 1 hour. Cool. Invert the cake onto a serving plate. Prick top with a wooden toothpick and drizzle the glaze evenly over top and sides. Allow cake to absorb glaze. Repeat this process as needed to use all of the glaze.

Glaze: Melt butter in saucepan. Stir in water and sugar. Boil 5 minutes, stirring constantly. Remove from heat. Stir in amaretto liqueur.

Serves 12

A Bundt pan works well for altitudes over 8,000 feet.

D
E
S
S
E
R
T
S

Chocolate Ganache Cake

CAKE

1	stick unsalted butter, room temperature
1	cup minus 3 tablespoons sugar
4	extra large eggs
1	16-ounce can chocolate syrup
1	tablespoon vanilla extract
1	cup all-purpose flour

FOR THE GANACHE

½	cup heavy cream
8	ounces semisweet chocolate chips
1	teaspoon instant coffee granules

Cake: Preheat oven to 345°F. Line a 9-inch round cake pan with parchment paper. In a mixing bowl, cream butter and sugar until smooth. Add eggs one at a time, mixing after each. Mix in chocolate syrup and vanilla extract. Add flour and mix until just combined - don't over beat. Pour into lined cake pan. Bake 45-60 minutes or until just set in the middle. Remove from oven and turn upside down on cake plate.

Ganache: Using a double boiler over simmering water, add the cream, chocolate chips, and coffee granules and heat until melted and until smooth. Pour over the plated cake. Serve with raspberries on top if desired.

Serves 8

Better Than Sex
German Chocolate Cake

3	tablespoons cocoa powder for cake pans instead of white flour
2¼	cups sifted cake flour
¾	teaspoon baking soda
½	teaspoon salt
4	ounces sweet baking chocolate, finely chopped
½	cup boiling water
1	cup plus 3 tablespoons buttermilk
1	teaspoon vanilla extract
2	sticks unsalted butter, room temperature
1¾	cups sugar, separated to 1½ cups and ¼ cup
5	large eggs, separated, room temperature
⅛	teaspoon cream of tartar

Preheat baking oven to 350°F or convection oven to 325°F. Before starting, make sure the eggs and butter are at room temperature. Read the directions before you get started. Grease and dust with cocoa powder the bottom of three 8x2-inch round cake pans. Then line the pans with parchment paper and grease and dust the paper.

Sift together the cake flour, baking soda, and salt. Set aside. Combine and stir the baking chocolate and boiling water until melted and set aside. Combine the buttermilk and vanilla extract and set aside.

In a large mixing bowl, beat the butter until creamy. Then add 1½ cups of sugar and beat on high speed for 4-6 minutes until the mixture becomes light in color. Beat in the egg yolks one at a time. Add the melted chocolate just until it is incorporated. Add the flour mixture in 3 parts, alternating with the buttermilk vanilla extract mixture in 2 parts, beating on low speed until smooth. Be sure to scrape the sides of the bowl with a spatula.

In another bowl, beat the egg whites and cream of tartar with an electric mixer on medium speed until very soft peaks form. Do not let the peaks reach the stiff stage. Then add the ¼ cup of sugar and continue to beat. Do not let the peaks become stiff, or you will have a dry cake. With a large spatula fold ¼ of the egg white mixture into the batter mixture and then fold in the remaining egg white mixture.

D
E
S
S
E
R
T
S

Divide the batter among the three cake pans and spread evenly. Bake until a wooden toothpick inserted into the center comes out clean, approximately 20 minutes. Place cake pan on a rack and let cool for about 10 minutes before removing from the pan. Slide a sharp knife around the cake to detach it from the pan. Invert the cake and peel off the parchment paper liners. Then let the cake cool right side up before frosting.

Serves 12

This recipe has taken time to perfect at 8,700 feet above sea level. Really, take the time to read the recipe before you get started. It is easy to make and well worth the effort. The cake is beautiful and tastes great, too. The preparation time for this cake is 45 minutes. Keep your eyes on it while baking as oven temperatures may vary.

195

German Chocolate Cake Frosting

2	cups sugar
2	cups evaporated milk
6	large egg yolks
2	sticks unsalted butter, cut into small pieces
2⅔	cups flaked sweetened dried coconut, toasted
2⅔	cups chopped pecans
25	whole pecans

Toast the coconut for about 3 minutes at 300°F. In a medium saucepan, combine sugar, evaporated milk, eggs, and butter. Cook, stirring constantly over medium heat until the mixture is bubbling around the edges. Reduce the heat to low and cook, stirring for 1-2 more minutes. Remove from heat and stir in the coconut and chopped pecans. Let it cool until able to spread easily.

Once the frosting is cooled, spread it all over the cake starting with the sides and then the top. Put whole pecans on the top of the cake starting along the top edge with the pointed ends facing toward the center of the cake. Repeat this step until you come to the center of the cake.

Enough to frost one 3-layer cake.

A fresh cherry or a maraschino cherry in the center looks pretty. A sparkler looks really spectacular lit up.

DESSERTS

Flourless Chocolate Cake

4 ounces fine quality, bittersweet chocolate (not unsweetened), chopped into small pieces
1 stick (½ cup) unsalted butter
¾ cup sugar
3 large eggs
½ cup unsweetened cocoa powder plus additional for dusting

Preheat oven to 375°F. Butter an 8-inch round baking pan. Line bottom with a round of wax paper and butter top side of paper. In a double boiler over simmering water, melt chocolate with butter, stirring until smooth.

Remove from heat and whisk sugar into chocolate mixture. Whisk in eggs. Sift ½ cup cocoa powder over chocolate mixture and whisk until just combined. Pour batter into pan and bake in middle of oven 20-25 minutes, or until top has formed a thick crust. Cool in pan on a rack for 5 minutes and invert onto a serving plate. To serve, dust cake with additional cocoa powder.

Serves 10-12

This cake is very rich. A small piece goes a very long way.

Cranberry Squares

1½ cups sugar
2 large eggs
¾ cup butter, melted and cooled
1 teaspoon almond extract
1½ cups flour
2 cups cranberries
½ cup chopped almonds

Preheat oven to 350°F. Butter a 9x9-inch square pan. Using an electric mixer wih a large bowl, beat sugar and eggs until thick and creamy for about 2 minutes. Beat in butter and extract. Add flour and stir by hand. Then stir in nuts and cranberries. Bake 1 hour, cool, and cut into squares.

Serves 12

Quick, easy, and delicious!

Volcano Cakes with Ganache Lava

CAKE
1   stick unsalted butter, room temperature
1   cup minus 2 tablespoons sugar
4   eggs, room temperature
2   cups chocolate syrup
1   cup all-purpose flour

GANACHE
¾   cup heavy cream
8   ounces semisweet chocolate chips
1   teaspoon instant coffee granules or 1 tablespoon unsweetened espresso
     Coffee-flavored or other flavor liqueur (optional)

Preheat the oven to 335°F. Butter and flour 18 muffin tins. Cream the butter and sugar together until light and fluffy. Add the eggs one at a time, and then mix in the chocolate syrup and vanilla extract. Add the flour and mix until just combined. Do not over-beat, or the cake will be tough.

Pour the batter into the muffin tins. Fill each cup about ¾ full. Bake for 24 minutes. Let cool for 5-10 minutes in the pan and then invert onto a plate or rack to finish cooling.

To make the ganache, place a double boiler over simmering water. Melt the chocolate chips, cream, and coffee until smooth and warm, stirring occasionally. If desired, you can stir in coffee liqueur or other liqueur to taste.

To finish, place each cupcake upside down on a plate and poke a well in the middle using the handle of a wooden spoon. Pour the warm ganache into the well, letting it overflow and run down the sides of the cake. Serve immediately.

Serves 18

DESSERTS

For cakes with lots of fat or chocolate,
try reducing the shortening by 1 to 2 tablespoons
and add an egg to prevent cake from falling.

Southern Charm Cake with Cream Cheese Frosting

CAKE

3   cups all-purpose flour, plus
      2 tablespoons
1   teaspoon baking soda
1   teaspoon salt
2   cups sugar, minus
      2 tablespoons
1   teaspoon ground cinnamon
3   large eggs, beaten
1   cup vegetable oil
1½ teaspoons vanilla extract
1   8-ounce can crushed pineapple,
      undrained
1   cup chopped pecans
2   cups chopped bananas

CREAM CHEESE FROSTING

½   cup (4 ounces) fat-free cream
      cheese, chilled
¼   cup butter, softened
1   teaspoon grated lemon rind
1   teaspoon vanilla extract
3½ cups confectioners' sugar
⅓   cup chopped pecans

Preheat oven to 350°. Combine flour, soda, salt, sugar, and cinnamon in a large bowl. Add eggs and oil, stirring until dry ingredients are moistened. Do not beat. Stir in vanilla extract, pineapple, pecans, and bananas.

Pour batter into a greased and floured Bundt pan. Bake for 25-30 minutes or until a wooden pick inserted in center comes out clean. Cool for 5 minutes and remove from pan. When cooled, spread the cake with cream cheese frosting and sprinkle with pecans. Store in refrigerator.

Cream Cheese Frosting: Beat cream cheese, butter, lemon, and vanilla extract at medium speed until smooth. Gradually add the sugar and beat at low speed until just blended.

Serves 12-16

Fill pans ⅓ to no more than ½ full to avoid
batter overflow caused by rapid cake expansion.

Italian Wedding Mini-Cakes

CUPCAKES

3	sticks unsalted butter, room temperature
2	cups minus 3 tablespoons sugar
5	extra large eggs, room temperature
1½	teaspoons vanilla extract
1½	teaspoons almond extract
3	cups all-purpose flour
1	teaspoon baking powder
½	teaspoon baking soda
½	teaspoon salt
1	cup plus 3 tablespoons buttermilk
14	ounces sweetened shredded coconut
	Chopped walnuts (optional)

CREAM CHEESE ICING

16	ounces cream cheese, room temperature
3	sticks unsalted butter, room temperature
1	teaspoon vanilla extract
½	teaspoon almond extract
1½	pounds confectioners' sugar, sifted

Preheat oven to 335°F. In a mixing bowl, cream butter and sugar until light and fluffy, about 5 minutes. With mixer running on low, add the eggs one at a time and scrape down bowl after each addition. Add the extracts and mix well. In a separate bowl, sift together the flour, baking powder, baking soda, and salt. Add half the flour mixture, all of the buttermilk, then the rest of the flour, mixing until just combined after each addition. Fold in 7 ounces of coconut. Line a muffin pan with liners and fill to the top with batter. Bake for approximately 22 minutes, until a wooden toothpick inserted in center comes out clean. Allow to cool in pan for 15 minutes then remove to rack.

Icing: Blend together cream cheese, butter, and extracts. Add sugar and mix until smooth. Frost the cupcakes and sprinkle with remaining coconut and/or chopped walnuts.

Serves 12

These cupcakes taste remarkably like Italian wedding cake, so instead of sprinkling coconut over the iced cupcakes you might want to chop up some walnuts and sprinkle those on top.

Old-Fashioned Cider Gingerbread Bundt Cake

2½ cups all-purpose flour, plus
    2 tablespoons
1 tablespoon ground ginger
1¾ teaspoons baking soda
1 teaspoon ground cinnamon
1 teaspoon ground cloves
¼ teaspoon salt
1 cup granulated sugar
¾ cup blackstrap molasses
¾ cup apple cider
½ cup apple butter
¼ vegetable oil
1 egg
1⅓ cups peeled and grated Granny
    Smith apple (about 1 apple)
1 tablespoon confectioners'
    sugar

Preheat oven to 350°F. In a bowl, combine flour, ginger, soda, cinnamon, cloves, and salt. In a separate bowl, combine granulated sugar, molasses, cider, butter, oil, and egg and beat at medium speed for about 2 minutes. Add flour mixture and beat until well blended. Add apple and beat well. Pour batter into a 12-cup Bundt pan coated with cooking spray and lightly floured. Bake for about 35-40 minutes until a wooden toothpick inserted in center comes out clean. Cool in pan for 5 minutes and then remove cake. Cool completely. Just before serving, sift confectioners' sugar over cake.

Serves 12-16

D
E
S
S
E
R
T
S

Rhubarb Cake

CAKE
½ cup butter
1½ cups minus 3 tablespoons
    brown sugar
1 beaten egg
1 teaspoon salt
¾ teaspoon baking soda
2¼ cups flour
1 cup plus 2 tablespoons
    buttermilk or goat milk
1 teaspoon vanilla extract
2 cups chopped rhubarb (stir in)

TOPPING
½ cup brown sugar
½ cup chopped nuts
1 teaspoon cinnamon

Preheat oven to 350°F. Mix all cake ingredients and pour into a greased and floured 9x13-inch pan. In a small bowl, mix topping ingredients and spread on top of cake mixture. Bake for 45 minutes.

Serves 12

Torta di Capezzana — Olive Oil Cake

3 eggs
2½ cups granulated sugar
1½ cups extra virgin olive oil
1½ cups milk
Grated zest of 3 oranges
2¼ cups unbleached all-purpose flour
½ teaspoon baking powder
½ teaspoon baking soda
Pinch of salt
Confectioners' sugar for dusting
1 orange, sliced for garnish

Preheat oven to 350°F. Butter and flour a 12-inch cake pan. In a large bowl, whisk together eggs and sugar until blended. Add olive oil, milk, and orange zest and mix well. In another bowl, stir together the flour, baking powder, baking soda, and salt. Add to the egg mixture, stirring just until blended. Do not over-mix. Pour the batter into the prepared pan. Bake until a wooden toothpick inserted in the center comes out clean, 50-55 minutes. Remove to a wire rack to cool completely. Loosen the sides with a knife and invert onto a serving plate. Dust the cake with confectioners' sugar and cut into 12 slices. Garnish the individual servings with fresh orange slices.

Serves 12

> This is a recipe from Tenuta di Capezzana,
> the Bonacossi estate in the hills west of Florence.

Puerto Rican Rum Cake

CAKE
½ cup chopped pecans
1 package yellow cake mix
1 3.4-ounce package instant vanilla pudding
4 eggs
½ cup cold water
½ cup vegetable oil
½ cup rum

GLAZE
¼ pound butter
¼ cup water
1 cup granulated sugar
½ cup rum

Preheat oven to 325°F. Grease and flour 10-inch tube or 12-cup Bundt pan. Sprinkle pecans over bottom of pan. Mix all cake ingredients together. Pour batter over pecans in pan. Bake one hour. Set on rack to cool. Invert on serving plate. Prick top of cake with toothpick or skewer. Drizzle and brush glaze evenly over top.

Glaze: In a saucepan, melt the butter. Stir in water and sugar. Boil 5 minutes, stirring constantly. Stir in rum.

Serves 8-12

Italian Orange Almond Cake

2 small seedless oranges, with peel
1 lemon, with peel
6 ounces almonds, finely chopped
6 eggs
½ teaspoon salt
1½ cups sugar
1 cup flour
2 teaspoons baking powder

Preheat oven to 350°F. Put the whole oranges and the whole lemon in a small saucepan and add water to cover. Heat to boiling, then reduce the heat, cover and simmer for 30 minutes. Drain and cool. Cut off the stem end of the oranges and lemon. Cut the citrus in quarters and chop finely, taking care to remove any seeds. Do not purée. Drain and set the fruit aside. (Save the juice for other uses.) Chop the almonds until almost fine crumbs.

In a food processor or the bowl of a mixer, beat the eggs and salt until very thick and light - 1 minute in the processor or 5 minutes in the mixer. Gradually add the sugar and beat until the sugar dissolves. Stir together the flour and baking powder. Add to the egg-sugar mixture. Mix until blended. Gently fold the chopped almonds and drained fruit into the egg-sugar-flour mixture until just blended. Do not over-mix. Turn the batter into a buttered 9-inch springform pan. Bake the cake about 1-1¼ hours or until a knife inserted near the center comes out clean. Cool the cake on a wire rack. Remove the sides of the pan when the cake is completely cool.

Serves 8-10

To prevent the top from becoming too brown, cover with foil after the first 15 minutes of baking and remove for the last 15 minutes.

D
E
S
S
E
R
T
S

Caramel Fondue Sauce. Two-third cup whipping cream, 1 (14-ounce) bag caramels, and ½-1 cup miniature marshmallows. Melt caramels in cream on low heat. Add marshmallows and stir until they are melted. Serve with apple wedges or drizzle on the Orange Almond Cake.

Schwarzwaldstårta

(Swedish Hazelnut Torte with Dark Chocolate)

NUT LAYERS

1½	cups hazelnuts (Filberts)
1¼	cups confectioners' sugar
1	tablespoon cornstarch
5	egg whites

FILLING

3	cups whipping cream (not ultra pasteurized)
½	cup roasted hazelnuts

FINISH DÉCOR AND GARNISH

1	bar of high quality semisweet dark chocolate
5	ounces or more of cocoa powder

Preheat oven to 375°F. Grind hazelnuts and mix with confectioners' sugar and cornstarch. Whip egg whites until fluffy. Blend into dry ingredients. On a buttered and floured baking sheet make three rounds of batter. Bake for about 10 minutes or until golden brown. Carefully loosen and set to cool.

For filling and to decorate: Whip cream and set aside enough to cover top and sides of cake. Mix the roasted ground hazelnuts in with remaining cream and fill in between cake layers. Cover with the rest of cream. Melt chocolate and lay out to cool on waxed paper (or parchment paper) in long strips. Cut into squares to decorate around the top of cake. Sprinkle with a little cocoa for final touch.

Serves 8-12

Coffee Liqueur Cookies

1	9-ounce package chocolate wafer cookies
½	pound blanched almonds, ground
⅓	cup unsweetened cocoa powder
¼	cup sugar
2	tablespoons instant coffee granules
⅓	cup coffee liqueur
½	cup light corn syrup
½	cup cinnamon sugar

Crush the chocolate wafer cookies into fine crumbs. Mix the cookie crumbs with the almonds, cocoa powder, and sugar. Dissolve the coffee granules in the liqueur and stir this along with the corn syrup into the cookie crumb mixture, blending well. Shape into ¾-inch balls and roll in the cinnamon sugar to coat. Store in the refrigerator.

Makes approximately 5 dozen cookies.

Ann's Lemon Melt-Aways

COOKIES

1	cup flour
⅔	cup cornstarch
1	cup butter
⅓	cup confectioners' sugar

FROSTING

¼	cup butter
⅛	teaspoon salt
2	tablespoons lemon juice
2	cups confectioners' sugar

Preheat oven to 350°F. Sift flour and cornstarch together. Cream butter and sugar. Then add dry ingredients. Drop by teaspoonful onto cookie sheet (or use auto cookie press). Bake 12-15 minutes.

Frosting: Cream all ingredients together. Frost cooled cookies.

Makes 24 cookies

204

D
E
S
S
E
R
T
S

Honey Cream-Filled Crescents

4	ounces cream cheese, softened
3	tablespoons honey
¼	cup sliced almonds or chopped pecans
1	8-ounce package refrigerated crescent dinner rolls
	Dash of ground cinnamon

Preheat oven to 375°F. Mix cream cheese and 2 tablespoons of the honey. Stir in almonds. Unroll crescent roll dough and separate into 8 triangles. Spread 1 rounded tablespoon cream cheese mixture onto each triangle. Roll each one up loosely, starting at shortest side of triangle, rolling to opposite point. Place rolls on ungreased baking sheet and curve each into crescent shape. Sprinkle with cinnamon. Bake 12-14 minutes or until golden brown. Serve rolls warm, drizzled with the remaining honey.

Serves 8

For a sweet and simple dessert, top with fresh berries and honey and garnish with whipped cream.

Soft Pumpkin Cookies

1	cup packed brown sugar
1	egg
½	cup margarine
1	teaspoon vanilla extract
1	15-ounce can unsweetened pumpkin
1½	teaspoons pumpkin pie spice
2½	cups flour
1	teaspoon baking soda
½	teaspoon salt
1	teaspoon baking powder
1	cup of raisins

Preheat oven to 350°F. In a mixing bowl, cream brown sugar, egg, margarine, and vanilla extract. Add pumpkin and pie spice. Then add flour, soda, salt, baking powder, and raisins. Drop by tablespoons onto greased cookie sheet. Bake for 12-15 minutes or until edges begin to brown.

Makes 24 cookies

Make your own vanilla concentrate by placing 2 split and chopped vanilla pods in 1 liter of vodka or bourbon. Shake the bottle once a day, let sit for 2-3 months.

Scotch Totties

⅔	cup butter, melted
4	cups of rolled oats
½	cup dark corn syrup
1	cup brown sugar
½	teaspoon salt
2	cups of chocolate chips
½	cup nuts

Preheat oven to 325°F. Pour hot butter over oatmeal. Add dark corn syrup, brown sugar, salt, chocolate chips, and nuts. Put in a hot buttered 9x13-inch pan. Bake for 15-20 minutes or until brown and bubbly. Allow to cool slightly, cut into squares.

Makes 12 bars

This recipe came from a woman who baked them for men overseas during wartime. They pack easily, don't spoil, and if they harden, dip them in hot tea or coffee. Yum!!

DESSERTS

Toffee Cookies

1 cup softened butter
1 cup brown sugar
1 teaspoon vanilla extract
1 egg yolk
2 cups flour
1 package of six plain chocolate candy bars
1 cup or more of finely crushed pecans

Preheat oven to 350°F. Cream the butter and brown sugar. Then add vanilla extract and egg yolk. Once these are creamed, gradually add the flour until mixture is smooth. Spread this onto a lightly buttered 9x12-inch cookie sheet. Bake for approximately 18 minutes. Watch closely as you don't want to burn this layer.

When baked, pull out of the oven. Break the 6 chocolate bars into small pieces and place all over the toffee. Let chocolate melt, then spread to evenly cover the surface of the toffee. Immediately sprinkle on the finely crushed pecans. Once complete, immediately cut into little squares about 1-2 inches each. Let the cookies cool fully before transferring to a tin for storage.

Makes 24-36 cookies

One tray full fills a medium size tin. However, these are so good when they first come out of the oven that you may only fill a smaller tin.

D
E
S
S
E
R
T
S

Although many sea level cookie recipes yield acceptable results at high altitudes, they often can be improved by a slight increase in baking temperature, a slight decrease in baking powder or soda, fat, and sugar and/or a slight increase in liquid ingredients and flour. Many cookie recipes contain a higher proportion of sugar and fat than necessary, even at low altitudes.

Toffee Triangles

CRUST
½   cup butter
½   cup brown sugar
1   large egg yolk
1½   cups flour

TOPPING
1   cup brown sugar
½   cup butter
¼   cup honey
½   cup heavy cream
3   cups chopped nuts

Preheat oven to 350°F. Line a 9x13-inch pan with foil extending on the short side. Mix all crust ingredients, except flour, until fluffy, then add flour. Press into the lined pan and bake for 15 minutes or until golden. In a saucepan, heat sugar, butter, and honey. Boil for 3 minutes. Remove from heat. Add heavy cream and nuts. Pour over crust. Bake for 24 minutes or until golden. Cool in pan. Lift foil to a cutting board. Cut 3 long strips. Cut the 3 long strips into 8 short strips making 24 squares. Cut each square crosswise to make a triangle.

Makes 48 triangles

D
E
S
S
E
R
T
S

Sister's Caramel Brownies

1   14-ounce package caramels, unwrapped
⅓   cup evaporated milk
1   package German chocolate cake mix
¾   cup butter, melted
⅓   cup evaporated milk
1   cup chopped nuts (optional)
6   ounces or 1 cup semisweet chocolate chips

Preheat oven to 350°F. In a small saucepan, combine caramels and milk over low heat until caramels have melted. Set aside. Grease and flour 9x13-inch pan. Combine cake mix, butter, and remaining milk. Add nuts and stir by hand. Press ½ of the dough into prepared pan. Bake for 6 minutes. Pour chocolate chips over the baked crust. Pour caramel mixture over the chips. Crumble remaining dough on top. Bake 15-18 minutes. Cool before cutting.

Makes 24 bars

Curried Sunflower Pine Nut Brittle

1	cup unsalted, untoasted sunflower seed kernels
½	cup unsalted, untoasted pine nuts
¾	teaspoon curry powder
⅛	teaspoon salt
1¼	cups sugar
¼	cup water
2	tablespoons light corn syrup

Line a baking sheet with foil and coat foil with cooking spray. Coat the flat surface of a metal spatula with cooking spray and set aside.

Heat a large nonstick skillet over medium-high heat. Add sunflower kernels and pine nuts. Cook until they release a toasted aroma (about 3 minutes), stirring frequently. Place in a bowl. Reheat the same pan, add curry powder, and cook until fragrant (about 30 seconds), stirring constantly. Add curry to kernels and pine nuts and stir to combine.

Combine sugar, water, and corn syrup in a saucepan. Bring mixture to a boil over medium-high heat, stirring occasionally until sugar dissolves. Continue to cook, without stirring, until the first sign of caramel fragrance (about 3 minutes). Remove from heat. Stir in kernels and pine nuts. Rapidly spread mixture to about ⅛-inch thickness onto prepared baking sheet using the prepared spatula. Cool completely and break into small pieces.

Serves 16

D
E
S
S
E
R
T
S

One Crust Apple Pie

6-8	apples, peeled, cored, and sliced
1	tablespoon sugar
1-2	teaspoons cinnamon
½	cup butter or margarine, melted
1	cup sugar
1	cup flour
1	egg
½	cup walnuts, chopped (optional)
	Pinch of salt

Preheat oven to 350°F. In a bowl, mix apples with sugar and cinnamon. Put apple mixture in a 9-inch pie pan. To make the crust, in a small bowl, mix butter or margarine, sugar, flour, egg, salt, and walnuts. Spread crust mixture over apples. Bake until golden brown, about 45 minutes.

Serves 8

Bavarian Apple Strudel

1   package phyllo dough
3   pounds tart apples
        Juice of 1 lemon
5   ounces raisins
5   tablespoons rum
3   ounces butter
1   cup sour cream
        Sugar and cinnamon to taste
1   cup milk
1   cup cream
        Confectioners' sugar

Preheat oven to 470°F. Butter a 9x13-inch baking pan, set aside. Peel, core, and quarter the apples. Cut them into thin slices and sprinkle with lemon juice to avoid discoloration. Brush the phyllo dough with warm melted butter. Dab the sour cream over the butter and distribute it evenly. Spread the apple slices over the dough in an even layer, stopping short about 1 inch from the edge of the dough. Sprinkle with the rum-soaked raisins, sugar, and cinnamon. Fold in the edges of the dough and, with the help of a towel, roll up the strudel loosely. Slide the strudel into the well-buttered baking pan. Proceed in the same manner with the second strudel, place alongside the first strudel.

Bring milk and cream to a boil and pour over the strudels in the pan. Place strudels in the oven and reduce the temperature to 420°F. Bake on middle rack of oven for 45-60 minutes. Cut into portions before serving and sprinkle with sifted sugar. Serve hot or cold.

Serves 8-10

DESSERTS

In contrast to the famous Apple Strudel of Vienna, which is baked on a baking sheet, its Munich counterpart is a juicy affair prepared in a baking dish. Apple Strudel may be stored in a freezer.

Blueberry Peach Tart

3   cups peaches, peeled, pitted, and sliced
½   cup blueberries
2   tablespoons sugar
1   tablespoon apricot preserves, melted
1   tablespoon sugar
1   pie crust (not frozen)

Preheat oven to 425°F. Line a baking sheet with foil or parchment paper. Roll pie crust to a 12-inch circle and put on the cookie sheet. Combine peaches, berries, and sugar and let sit for a few minutes. Arrange fruit mixture in center of the dough. Pull edges toward the center, but not to touch, gently pressing folds together. Spread preserves on crust. Bake for 10 minutes. Reduce heat to 350°F and bake 20 more minutes. Sprinkle with sugar immediately when removing from oven. Cool slightly before slicing and serving.

Serves 8

Very easy and elegant dessert. Serve with gelato or whipped cream.

Melt-In-Your-Mouth Cranberry Pie

2   cups fresh cranberries, picked over
½   cup chopped walnuts
1½ cups sugar
2   large eggs
1   cup all-purpose flour
1   stick (½ cup) unsalted butter, melted
¼   cup vegetable shortening, melted

Preheat oven to 325°F. Butter a 10-inch (1½-quart) pie plate. Arrange cranberries on bottom of plate. Sprinkle cranberries with walnuts and ½ cup of sugar. With electric mixer, beat eggs in bowl. Gradually add remaining cup of sugar to eggs and beat until light yellow and frothy. Add flour, butter, and shortening and beat until smooth. Spoon batter over cranberries. Bake in middle of oven for 1 hour or until top is golden.

Serves 8

Cranberry and Apple Cobbler

5   cups baking apples, peeled, cored, and sliced
1¼ cups sugar
1   cup fresh cranberries
3   tablespoons quick tapioca
½   teaspoon ground cinnamon
1   cup water
2   tablespoons butter or margarine
¾   cup flour
2   tablespoons sugar
1   teaspoon baking powder
⅛   teaspoon salt
¼   cup butter or margarine
3   tablespoons milk

Preheat oven to 375°F. In large saucepan, mix apple slices, 1¼ cups sugar, cranberries, tapioca, cinnamon, and water. Let stand 5 minutes. Cook over medium heat, stirring constantly, until mixture comes to a full boil. Pour into 2-quart baking dish. Dot with 2 tablespoons butter. In large bowl, mix flour, 2 tablespoons sugar, baking powder, and salt. Cut in ¼ cup butter until mixture resembles coarse crumbs. Stir in milk until soft dough forms. Drop dough by tablespoons onto hot apple mixture. Bake 30 minutes or until topping is golden brown. Serve warm with whipped topping or vanilla ice cream, if desired.

Serves 8

To fill a 13x9x2-inch baking dish: Multiply recipe by 1½ times, using 1 bag cranberries and about 8 apples. Best apples to use: Braeburn, Fuji, Gala, Pink Lady or Golden Delicious.

D
E
S
S
E
R
T
S

> When using fresh apples, do not cut pieces too thin.
> Larger chunks will hold together and have more apple flavor.

Double Crust Peach Cobbler

8 cups peeled, pitted, and sliced peaches
2 cups sugar
3 tablespoons all-purpose flour
½ teaspoon nutmeg
1 teaspoon almond extract
⅓ cup butter, melted
   Pastry for double crust pie

Preheat oven to 475°F. In a large mixing bowl, combine peaches, sugar, flour, and nutmeg. Set aside until syrup forms. Bring peach mixture to a boil and cook over low heat 10 minutes. Don't overcook. Remove from heat and add almond extract and butter, stirring well.

On a lightly floured board, roll out half of pastry to ⅛-inch thickness and cut into a 10x8-inch rectangle. Spoon half of peaches into a lightly buttered baking dish. Top with pastry. Bake for 12 minutes or until golden brown. Spoon remaining peaches over baked pastry.

While first pastry is baking, roll out remaining pastry and cut into ½-inch strips. When first baking is done, arrange strips in lattice design over peaches. Lower oven temperature to 375°F. Return cobbler to the oven for 10-15 minutes or until top is lightly browned. Serve warm with ice cream.

Serves 8-10

To make the crust golden brown, brush the pastry with an egg beaten with a little water.

DESSERTS

Hot Fudge Sauce

¾ cup confectioners' sugar
1½ squares bittersweet chocolate
3 tablespoons butter or margarine
¾ cup evaporated milk
   Dash of salt
½ teaspoon vanilla

Using a double boiler set over boiling water, mix butter, chocolate, and evaporated milk and simmer until well mixed. Stir frequently, so the chocolate does not burn. Add vanilla and mix well. After these ingredients are blended well, add the confectioners' sugar and salt. Keep stirring until the fudge sauce thickens, about 5-10 minutes.

Serves 4-6

Perfect Pecan Pie

1   9-inch baked pie shell
1   cup packed dark brown sugar
6   tablespoons unsalted butter,
        cut into 1-inch pieces
3   large eggs
½   teaspoon salt
1   tablespoon vanilla extract
¾   cup light corn syrup
2   cups pecans, toasted and
        chopped into small pieces

Preheat oven to 275°F. Adjust oven rack to center position. Place pie shell in oven to warm while you prepare the filling being careful not to overbake. In a medium heatproof bowl, melt the butter. Mix in sugar and salt with wooden spoon until butter is absorbed. Beat in eggs. Add corn syrup and vanilla extract. Place bowl over hot water and stir until mixture is shiny and warm to the touch, about 130°F. Remove from heat and stir in pecans.

Pour mixture into the warm shell and bake until center feels set yet soft, like gelatin, when gently pressed, at least 55-65 minutes. Cover crust with foil if the edges get too brown. Transfer pie to rack and let cool completely, at least 4 hours. Serve pie at room temperature or warm, with lightly sweetened whipped cream or vanilla ice cream.

Serves 8

This recipe is fussy, fussy, but it is so worth it! Be forewarned: You really do need to follow the recipe exactly, so use a candy thermometer. Also, the altitude does something interesting to this pie. You've probably heard that you're supposed to use less sugar when cooking at high altitudes. Using the amount of sugar called for in this recipe makes a delicious pie, but it's sweeter than the pecan pie you may be used to. Keep that in mind, and if you aren't into really sweet pie you might want to leave out a tablespoon or two of the sugar.

D
E
S
S
E
R
T
S

Old-Fashioned Pumpkin Pie

PIE

1	28-ounce can pumpkin
1½	cups brown sugar, firmly packed
4	extra large eggs, well beaten
3	tablespoons melted butter
2	tablespoons dark molasses or dark corn syrup
1	tablespoon pumpkin pie spice
1½	teaspoons salt
1¼	cups whole milk
2	unbaked pie crusts

PUMPKIN PIE SPICE

2	teaspoons cinnamon
¾	teaspoon ginger
½	teaspoon ground nutmeg

Preheat oven to 450°F. Combine pumpkin, brown sugar and add beaten eggs. Mix well. Add melted butter, dark molasses, pumpkin pie spice, and salt. Gradually stir in the milk, making sure the mixture is thoroughly blended.

Prepare pie crusts in pie pans and pour pumpkin filling into the crusts.

Bake for 15 minutes. Reduce heat to 340°F and leave oven door ajar for a few minutes to quickly cool oven. Bake for 50-60 minutes or until a wooden toothpick comes out clean when inserted in the center of the filling. Since ovens vary slightly, be sure to check pies every so often and watch the crust. Cover crust edges with aluminum foil if crust starts to get too brown.

Makes 2 pies

This is the mother of all pumpkin pie recipes. It takes a little more time than those quickie pumpkin pies, but the reward is a truly wonderful pie!

214

D
E
S
S
E
R
T
S

Chantilly Cream

1	cup heavy cream
2	teaspoons vanilla extract
3	tablespoons bourbon
2	tablespoons orange liqueur
½	cup sugar
3	tablespoons sour cream

Blend cream, vanilla extract, bourbon, and orange liqueur using a mixer. Slowly add sugar and sour cream, blend 3 more minutes until stiff.

Makes 2 cups

Granny's Bread Pudding with Rum Sauce

PUDDING
9	slices of white or French bread
1¼	cups sugar, divided
1	12-ounce can of evaporated milk
2	cups whole milk
1	teaspoon of vanilla extract
4	eggs, separated
½	cup butter, melted
½	cup golden raisins
½	cup pecans, coarsely chopped

RUM SAUCE
1	cup of sugar
1	cup evaporated milk
3	tablespoons butter
1	cup whole milk
1½	tablespoons cornstarch
2	ounces rum

Bread pudding: Preheat oven at 450°F. In a large bowl, break bread into small pieces. Mix with 1 cup of sugar, evaporated milk, whole milk, egg yolks, melted butter, and vanilla extract. Add pecan pieces and raisins. Pour into a greased 10x8x2-inch casserole dish and bake for 30 minutes. Remove from oven and make meringue.

Meringue: Beat egg whites with remaining ¼ cup of sugar until stiff. Cover pudding with meringue and re-bake for 3-4 minutes until golden brown.

Rum Sauce: In a double boiler, stir together evaporated and whole milk, sugar and butter. When hot and sugar is dissolved, mix the cornstarch with a little water to dissolve. Add the cornstarch mixture to the pot. Stir until the sauce thickens. Remove from the heat and add the rum. Drizzle over bread pudding before serving.

Serves 12

215

D
E
S
S
E
R
T
S

To vary the recipe you can add cinnamon and nutmeg, omit the meringue, drizzle with a whiskey sauce, and top with Chantilly Cream. A favorite dessert served at the Platte Canyon Grille Restaurant in Bailey, Colorado.

Whiskey Sauce
½ cup sugar
½ cup water
3 cups bourbon
In a small saucepan, dissolve sugar in boiling water over high heat. Remove from heat. Add bourbon and ignite alcohol. When flame stops, sauce is ready to pour over pudding.

March Moon Madness

(Panettone Bread Pudding)

5	large eggs
1	8-ounce container heavy cream or soy creamer
½	stick butter
1	large Italian fruit bread (Panettone)

Preheat oven to 350°F. Butter a 9x13-inch glass dish and set aside. Break eggs into large bowl, add cream, and whisk until well mixed. Cut bread into 1-inch slices, crumble into egg and cream mixture, and mix thoroughly. Mixture will be quite thick. Pour into buttered glass dish and spread evenly. Cut remaining butter into chunks and sprinkle over mixture. Bake for 40 minutes or until knife inserted in center comes out clean. Allow to sit for 30 minutes or more and then serve as is or with cream.

Serves 8

Don't worry how stale the cake may be, just let the mixture soak a little longer.

Bobbie's Brownie Pudding

1	cup flour
2	teaspoons baking powder
½	teaspoon salt
¾	cup granulated sugar
¼	cup cocoa
½	cup milk
1	teaspoon vanilla extract
2	tablespoons shortening, melted
1	cup chopped walnuts or pecans
¾	cup brown sugar
2	tablespoons cocoa
1¾	cups hot water

Preheat oven to 350°F. In a mixing bowl, sift together flour, baking powder, salt, granulated sugar, and cocoa. Add milk, vanilla extract, and shortening and mix until smooth. Add nuts. Pour into greased 8x8-inch square cake pan. Mix brown sugar and cocoa and sprinkle over batter. Pour hot water over entire batter. Do not stir. Bake 40-45 minutes.

Serves 8-10

The brownie mixture rises to the top during baking, with a wonderful fudge sauce underneath.

Mocha Pot de Crème

1   6-ounce package semisweet chocolate chips
¼   cup sugar
1   tablespoon instant coffee
     Pinch of salt
1   large egg
1   teaspoon vanilla extract
1¼   cups light cream, heated carefully
¼   cup coffee-flavored liqueur (optional)
     Whipped cream or ice cream to garnish

Measure all ingredients except liqueur and whipping cream in a blender jar, adding hot cream last. Blend at high speed for 2 minutes. Pour into serving glasses, ramekins, or teacups and refrigerate 4 hours or until firm. Top with whipped cream, flavored with liqueur of your choice, or vanilla ice cream.

Serves 6

Easy Tiramisu Dessert

1   10.75-ounce package frozen pound cake, thawed and cut into 9 slices
¾   cup strong-brewed coffee, room temperature
1   cup sugar
½   cup chocolate syrup
1   8-ounce package mascarpone cheese or cream cheese, softened
2   cups whipping cream
2   1.4-ounce bars chocolate-covered toffee candy, chopped

Arrange cake slices in bottom of 11x7-inch rectangular baking dish, cutting cake slices if necessary to cover bottom of dish. Drizzle coffee over cake. Beat sugar, chocolate syrup, and cheese in a large bowl with electric mixer on medium speed until smooth. Add whipping cream and beat on medium speed until light and fluffy. Spread over cake. Sprinkle with candy. Cover and refrigerate at least 1 hour but no longer than 24 hours to set the dessert and blend the flavors.

Serves 12

If using a 9x13-inch pan, use two pound cakes and increase the rest of the recipe by half with the exception of the candy bars. This is quick and easy to make and delicious!

DESSERTS

Aunt Enza's Tiramisu

1   cup unsweetened espresso
3   eggs, separated
⅓   cup sugar, tablespoon
1½   cups mascarpone, softened
2   tablespoons Marsala
     (optional)
8   ounces ladyfingers
     Unsweetened cocoa or
     bittersweet chocolate

Prepare espresso and cool completely. Separate eggs and discard 1 egg white. Beat 2 egg whites with 1 tablespoon sugar until it forms soft peaks. In another bowl, beat egg yolks with remaining sugar until thick and pale yellow. Add mascarpone and Marsala (if using) to the egg yolk mixture and blend until well combined. Lightly fold egg whites into the mascarpone.

Dip ladyfingers in espresso and line the bottom of a 2-quart loaf pan with ⅓ of the cookies. Cover with ⅓ of the mascarpone and a dusting of cocoa. Continue building, making 3 layers of cookies topped with 3 layers of mascarpone. To finish, dust with cocoa or chopped-up/shaved chocolate. Refrigerate at least two hours.

Serves 6

I once did a tiramisu cook-off for some friends and made three different recipes at one time. This one was the hands-down winner. All tasters agreed that this was the best tiramisu they've ever tasted and that included an individual who claims that tiramisu is his absolute favorite dessert and one who spent a year in Italy. This version even pleased my husband, who is a pickier eater than any 2-year-old ever was.

218

Quick and Easy Strawberry Bavarian

1   10-ounce package frozen
    strawberries
2   envelopes gelatin
¼   cup cold whole milk
¼   cup sugar
2   eggs
1   heaping cup of crushed ice
1   cup heavy cream
    Fresh strawberries to garnish

Defrost berries, drain, and reserve the juice. Heat ½ cup of the strawberry juice to simmer. Place milk in food processor (using the steel blade), sprinkle gelatin over milk, and let soften a few minutes. Add hot juice. Process about 5 seconds. Add sugar and eggs and process 5 seconds. Add berries and process for 5 seconds. Add ice and cream. Process until the ice is melted. Pour into serving dishes and chill. Garnish with fresh strawberry slices.

Serves 4

DESSERTS

Above 5,000 feet (1,523m), temperatures obtained with a double boiler are not high enough for maximum gelatinization of starch. Therefore, use direct heat rather than a double boiler.

High Altitude Cooking Tips

What is high altitude?

Areas that are 3,500 feet above sea level are considered to be high-altitude areas. Therefore, cooking in these conditions demand certain adjustments to recipes, ingredients and technique in order to produce the desired outcome.

- All cooking processes are directly affected by atmospheric pressure.

- At sea level, water boils at 212 degrees, but on mountaintops and other high-altitude regions, the boiling point is much lower.

- For about every 500 feet of ascent, the boiling point is lowered by about 1 degree.

- At a 7,000-foot elevation, water would boil at about 198 degrees. Because the water is boiling at a lower temperature, it would take longer to cook food by boiling.

What about Puddings and Cream-Pie Fillings?

Above 5,000 feet, temperatures obtained with a double boiler are not high enough for maximum gelling. Therefore, use direct heat rather than a double boiler.

Can We Bake Bread Successfully?

This is where altitude issues have the most pronounced effect. At high altitudes, the rising period is shortened. Since the development of a good flavor in bread partially depends on the length of the rising period, it is a good idea to maintain that period. Punching down the dough twice gives time for the flavor to develop. Additionally, flours tend to be drier and are able to absorb more liquid so less flour may be needed to make the dough the proper consistency.

And for the All-Important Baking...

Here are some conversion tips that will help convert standard recipes to those that can be used for high-altitude baking:

- Use 5% more flour to disperse the leavening action and slow down the rapid rise.

- Use 20% more water to counterbalance the rapid evaporation of liquids at high altitudes and the extra flour added to the mixture.

- Bake cakes about 25 degrees higher to help "set" the cake's crust

- Reduce baking time by about 20% to prevent overbaking at the higher temperatures.

- Use cold water and large, cold eggs to give cakes extra strength.

- Remove top oven rack to prevent cake from sticking to it, since high-altitude cakes rise more.

- Have oven clibrated by a serviceperson periodically, since some thermostats are affected by the altitude.

Sources: The Crisco Kitchen (www.crisco.com)

Colorado State University Cooperative Extension Resource Center (www.cerc.colostate.edu)

Index

INDEX

222

223

I
N
D
E
X

224

I
N
D
E
X

225

I
N
D
E
X

227

228

I N D E X

229

I
N
D
E
X

INDEX

231

NOTES

To order additional copies of **Colorado Elevations**, please fill in the coupon below.

Mail to: **Colorado Elevations**
        c/o Conifer Newcomers and Neighbors
        PO Box 1027
        Conifer, CO 80433

Please send me _____ copies of **Colorado Elevations** at $21.95 per copy, plus $5.95 postage and handling per book. Colorado residents add $4.16 sales tax.

Enclosed is my check or money order for $_____.

Please Print:
Name _____

Address _____

City _____ State _____ ZIP _____

All proceeds from the sale of the cookbook go to the projects approved by the Conifer Newcomers and Neighbors.

Mail to: **Colorado Elevations**
        c/o Conifer Newcomers and Neighbors
        PO Box 1027
        Conifer, CO 80433

Please send me _____ copies of **Colorado Elevations** at $21.95 per copy, plus $5.95 postage and handling per book. Colorado residents add $4.16 sales tax.

Enclosed is my check or money order for $_____.

Please Print:
Name _____

Address _____

City _____ State _____ ZIP _____

All proceeds from the sale of the cookbook go to the projects approved by the Conifer Newcomers and Neighbors.

REORDER ADDITIONAL COPIES

To order additional copies of **Colorado Elevations**, please fill in the coupon below.

Mail to: **Colorado Elevations**
　　　　c/o Conifer Newcomers and Neighbors
　　　　PO Box 1027
　　　　Conifer, CO 80433

Please send me _____ copies of **Colorado Elevations** at $21.95 per copy, plus $5.95 postage and handling per book. Colorado residents add $4.16 sales tax.

Enclosed is my check or money order for $_____.

Please Print:
Name _____

Address _____

City _____ State _____ ZIP _____

All proceeds from the sale of the cookbook go to the projects approved by the Conifer Newcomers and Neighbors.

Mail to: **Colorado Elevations**
　　　　c/o Conifer Newcomers and Neighbors
　　　　PO Box 1027
　　　　Conifer, CO 80433

Please send me _____ copies of **Colorado Elevations** at $21.95 per copy, plus $5.95 postage and handling per book. Colorado residents add $4.16 sales tax.

Enclosed is my check or money order for $_____.

Please Print:
Name _____

Address _____

City _____ State _____ ZIP _____

All proceeds from the sale of the cookbook go to the projects approved by the Conifer Newcomers and Neighbors.

REORDER ADDITIONAL COPIES